Art, Culture & Gender

(The Indian Psyche)

Art, Culture & Gender

(The Indian Psyche)

S.T. Janetius

Mishil & Js, Thrissur

2016

First Printing: September 9, 2016
Mishil & Js Publishers, Thrissur

(Cover Photo: Equestrian Statue at Ranganathaswamy Temple, Srirangam.
Courtesy Shilpa, S.T.)

International Standard Book Number issued by
Amazon CreateSpace Independent Publishing Platform

ISBN-13: 9781537075341

ISBN-10: 1537075349

Psychology of Art and Culture
Culture and Psychology
Sex and Gender Issues
Consumer Psychology
Cyber Culture
Sex Taboos and Indian Society

Dedicated

to my

Psychology Students

The author is grateful to the following Scholars
for their valuable contribution.

Alemayehu, T.
Amrutha, M.S.
Ashwanth, K.
Govindarajan, P.
Manoj, T.
Mini, T.C.
Ravishankar, D.
Shilpa, S.T.
Willington, J.P.

Contents

Acknowledgments

I acknowledge my colleagues and students who are supportive of all my initiatives in understanding human behaviour. They keep an open mind to creativity and innovation without which no progress, development, and new thinking could be achieved.

Preface

While preparing a syllabus for psychology, a seminar paper was proposed to orient students to the application of psychology to current social context. Students responded positively to the themes Art, Culture, Gender and Human Behaviour. They also identified other adolescent issues like Cyberpsychology and Consumer Behaviour. This work gets its inspiration from two seminars organised by the students of psychology. The papers in the book reflect the changing Indian culture and modern Indian Psyche in various aspects.

Art, Culture and Gender issues reflect the human psyche down through the history. The identity of a person comes from family, community, country, land, culture and spirituality. One can't understand an individual removed from that. India is a multicultural, tolerant society with its complex traditions, beliefs and thinking, which is distressed by various socio-political and religious elements today. However, the glorious India is admired for its tolerance and multiculturalism. Due to pressure groups and fanatic outfits emerging in the society, India is slowly losing its original social outlook and tend to move towards a bigoted society. Multiculturalism is a beauty, as we see different flowers in a garden. The fascist ideology that is often propagated by fundamentalist groups spoils this beauty in the Indian society. In this regard, India needs some dynamic personalities who can propagate, educate and inculcate the glorious values of humanism and work for tolerance and harmony.

I would like to thank the students *Aksa, Alimiyan, Ann Varsha, Gowthami, Hashir,* and *Naveen* for their efforts taken in this regard and the other scholars who worked with them in their endeavours to create an awareness to enlighten the young minds for a better Indian society.

Dr Janetius
Director, Centre for Counselling and Guidance
Sree Saraswathi Thyagaraja College, Pollachi

Introduction

Culture & Parenting[1]

Here is a classic scene from a home: a young mother with an eight-month-old baby attempting to walk. The baby stands up and takes a step. The mother is excited and decides to leave the kid on his/her own. The mother moves away and tells the baby, come on baby ... stand up... come on baby ... stand up. The baby attempts to stand up and succeeds. The mother then encourages the baby to take a step forward. And then showing her arms invites the baby to walk across the room or halfway through the room. The baby slowly learns to take steps and walks. Then the baby falls while attempting to walk and starts crying as the pain seeps into the muscles.

Let me take you to a house in Middle-East country. The mother goes to the child picks up the baby and consoles him/her. The mother says: "it is okay, it is part of the growing up process, and you need to fall to learn to walk. Just stand up and try walking again". The baby indeed has been crying but slowly goes quiet watching the mother's expression. The mother now puts the baby down and encourages him/her to attempt the walking. I now take you to an Indian house. The mother runs towards the child with a panic stricken face and with a mix of sadness and anger. The mother says to the baby: 'don't cry, my baby. This floor is bad and let me beat the floor. Let me beat the

---

[1]**Manoj** who penned the Introduction is a trainer and inspirational speaker and a management guru.

floor for hurting my baby. Sorry … sorry … let me beat the floor'. The baby continues crying till s/he feels a game going, with the mother beating the floor and stops crying. Looks at the mother's face and expression!

Parenting is different in different parts of the world. Cultures differ, things happen differently, and the way of expressing a situation is different. Agreed. But, falling is part of growing up. Getting hurt and wounds are indeed part of a child's life. You want to learn to walk, please expect to fall a couple of times. It happens for learning to run too. It is how it is. So, why blame a floor for a fall? Well, the Indian baby learns to blame a 3rd party for something that s/he attempts to learn or improve in his life. The other baby learns to accept challenges and falls in an attempt to move forward.

Always remember that it is extremely difficult to preach this to a mother but what we described here is quite common in many homes, many cultures and countries. Regardless of the way you handle the situation, the baby learns one behaviour or the other, i.e., to take responsibility for your life or blame it on a third party. The key objective of being a parent is to have a sense of family, a symbol of love, answering to the call of creation and continuing the family lineage. Some parents might say that they want their children to do better in life than them and achieve better. Is it something that is easy to achieve or is there a quick guide to parents? The blue book?

Nature-Nurture Controversy[2]: It is to be noted that parents from medical background produce a child with extraordinary swimming

---

[2] The Nature-Nurture (heredity vs. environment; biology vs. sociology) debate in psychology is concerned with the extent to which particular aspects of behaviour are a product of either inherited (genetic) or acquired (learned) characteristics. Nature is what we think of as pre-wiring and is influenced by genetic inheritance and other biological factors whereas nurture is the result of exposure, experience and learning on an individual after conception. It is proven that certain physical characteristics are biologically determined. For example, the colour of the eyes, pigmentation of the skin and even certain diseases that include mental disorders. Those who adopt an extreme hereditary position are generally categorized as nativists and the other group is the environmentalists, also known as empiricists.

skills or parents from accounting background give birth to a child excelling in Piano. Indeed, there are doctors born in the family of doctors or a teacher born in a family of teachers. Is it the DNA driving the end result for a child or is it the upbringing? Dating back to mid 20th century there has been so many experiments to prove the theory of DNA versus upbringing. Let us not stir the age-old Heredity – Environment dispute among psychologists, philosophers, theologians, and theorists of consciousness as to the source of the creation of human personality started since the time of the great Greek physician Hippocrates (460-377 B.C.) More consistent information about the biological basis of human behaviour can be gathered from twin studies. Of the two kinds of twins (dizygotic & monozygotic), the identical (monozygotic) twins display remarkable behavioural similarities. Twin studies have also attempted to elucidate the genetic basis of intelligence, which, according to many psychologists, is not one trait, but a cluster of distinct traits. Generally, these studies indicate that identical twins reared in different families show a high correlation in IQ scores. However, scientists still do not know how intelligence is inherited and what specific aspects of intelligence can be linked to genetic factors. Leave aside this controversy, coming to our theme, is there anywhere you go and find a parent telling his child about working hard to be a good student or getting good grades? Well, I have seen many. So, motivating the child or putting pressure on the child, is the key to success.

Let me take you to a small story of a mother and a son meeting me at a conference seeking advice. So I spoke at the University campus for potential students and parents. The topic was *Goal setting as the Step to Success*. I spoke the importance of students being able to set a goal and how this helps in achieving success in the University and generally in life. In the first two seats of the conference, I noticed a mother and son keenly listening to my speech with a smile. After the conference, they approached me and she asked for some private time. I took permission from the Principal of the college to use her room for a small one on one session with the mother – son duo. The mother explained that she is very keen on her son to join the University College to attend a bachelor's degree but she is not very sure because according to her the son, he does not show any interest or excitement. Instead of just passing a judgment, I decided to deep dive and understand their common problem as well as differences. This led me to a long discussion which revealed a very interesting behaviour pattern.

Let me explain the mother's daily chores from 4pm to 9pm. The son returns from the high school at 5pm; he comes straight to sit on a chair in front of TV to watch one program after another. The son doesn't bother to change his clothes and does that only when he is about to go to bed. The mother prepares the dinner and the son eats dinner while watching TV. The son stops watching TV at 9pm, quietly retreats to his room, changes into night clothes and goes to sleep. The mother is concerned that the son does not read any of the school books or attempts to do any homework or practices any of the lessons. The mother thinks that the son is not interested in studies and she wonders how this pattern of behaviour will help the son to get through his bachelor's degree. The son says he is interested in certain TV programs (serials) thus making it a habit of watching the program regularly. He considers this as a part of relaxing after a long day at school. He didn't conclusively say he didn't like school yet he is very much willing to work hard to earn a living. There are the two sides of the story with different reasons but the common interest isn't missing. I applied my theory of goal setting.

Everyone talks about the importance of goal setting but nobody tells you how to set a goal. So the *how* part is the key to define, agree and follow through.

Let us go back to our story and see how we can set a goal for this son. The first part of the exercise starts with a small sacrifice. The time starts at 5pm when the son returns home from school and ends at 9pm. When I asked the son about his favourite program during these 4 hours he didn't have a certain answer. But he agreed that some of the timeslots weren't all that interesting. That was my breakthrough to get in with a goal setting program. The son agreed to sacrifice 30 minutes of the 4-hour time slot for reading some of the school material. The word sacrifice is a big word but it is often used in our families. Life in our families is all about sacrifices.

I looked up at the dictionary for the meaning of sacrifice. The original meaning of the word in the dictionary says 'an act of slaughtering an animal or person or surrendering a possession as an offering to God or to a divine or supernatural figure'. This made me wonder whether we should ever use the word sacrifice in our families as a way of expression. Compromises or alternate arrangements should replace the word sacrifice in our families.

Back to the story about the son, so I continued checking on the son's progress with the 'alternate arrangement'. The mother confessed that it was difficult for the son to adjust the new schedule to avoid watching TV for 30 minutes instead of reading up school topics. Well, he achieved it in 3 weeks' period and he was easily doing his 30 minutes' school work before returning to his watching TV schedule. By the way, the son was excited to tell me that he achieved what I asked him to do. He felt good, satisfied and he had a sense of achievement. I then asked the boy whether he could find another time slot for 30 minutes to read up more. He went through the TV Program and hesitantly pointed out another 30-minute time slot where he could potentially add to his school work program. I checked up on them after 3 months only to learn that the son is now spending 1 hour for school work.

The story has a success embedded in it. but doesn't guarantee any success for the son in pursuing his bachelor's degree. But let me summarize, how to set goals in life. The first part really is to deep dive into the subject to understand the problem. The problem may not be a right word; we need to know what the need for goal setting is. The second step is to set a small goal that can be easily achieved. The boy set a small goal (with a help) the mother followed up to ensure that the son reached the goal of reading for 30 minutes despite the struggle. The next step was to double the goal (double the timing) and again indeed the son achieved that too. On the other hand, this story also makes a coy reference to whether DNA or upbringing culture is important in achieving success or not. I will just add to this interesting angle the theory that what the mind can conceive, it can achieve. So this is leading me to a very strong emphasis on upbringing and motivation to the children.

The parenting culture[3] needs to be checked. How often do we motivate the child? Well, taking a bath doesn't keep our body clean for more than a day, so that is why it is recommended daily. The same is for motivation. A child who is motivated daily is likely to have the best results in life and achievement. How do we motivate the child and what do we say and what context is best? I leave that really to the parent and child. An open minded talk to the child is best recommended thus opening up different talents, thoughts, and dreams into the forefront.

We wouldn't have a *Sachin Tendulkar, Vijai, AR Rahman, Karan Johar or Adnan Sami* if their parents didn't allow them to follow their dreams. Their parents didn't stress their children for the schooling or degrees or anything. A child's mind is like how a butterfly is. It is beautiful, colourful and such a free soul. It wanders the beautiful flower gardens, looks for sweet flower buds, drinks the juice and gives all of us such joy. Let go of your child's dreams and thoughts. Let it wander, let it dream and let it form thoughts of its own. The child then has a way to experiment a sports skill or a music skill thus moving away from a conventional strict thought process. Give the confidence in everything they do and everything they want to do, you never know whether we have the Vijay Antony[4] in the house.

Interestingly enough, there is a psychological element to the fate – destiny myth. Based on the family you were born in, one chooses a

---

[3] Psychologists point out that in human species, maternal instinct is more natural and universal. The urge to look after and care for one's offspring is a basic trait of mothers/parents among all cultures around the globe. However, instinct doesn't offer any guidance to mothers or parents, how to take care of one's children. The various ways parents think and act upon their own children's development comes from the experience of their own parents and their customs or practices of care which need not be the correct one.

[4] Vijay Antony is a South Indian music composer, playback singer, and actor from Tamil Nadu who holds a degree in Visual Communication from Loyola College, Chennai. He made his debut as a Music Director in 2005 and in 2009 won the Cannes Golden Lion for his Nakka Mukka song. In 2012, he made his acting debut; both his first two movies were sleeper hits. His use of many incomprehensible words in the Tamil film songs together with Kuthu Paatu and rap mix in song compositions made him a special music director, loved by youngsters.

religion. Isn't religion a big part of deciding the fate – destiny – action trilogy? Well, there is a certain truth in religions influencing the trilogy. Well, unless one exercises his freewill to change the programming of the belief system. So how does the fate – destiny feature into this elaborate discussion on psyche? The main element to remember is to go back to taking responsibility versus blaming a third party for a result or an incident. This leads to a natural suggestion that fate doesn't exist but rather everything is a result of a set of actions. Fate can be influenced and is a human intervention.

By no means does my concept overrule the theory of divine intervention. Divine intervention is absolutely in existence but rather a disclaimer and definition of terminology will be in order. So to simplify the matter, we must believe that the mind is one of the most powerful sources in the world and in the Universe. Without this belief, we cannot move forward. Did I use the word, belief?, yes I did. So in terms of definitions, whether you call it Universe or God or the supreme one, it is all one. The principle of oneness is absolutely the foundation of the theory. The mind dreams, mind constantly believes in the dream, achievement of the dream and have an absolute belief about the outcome. It is thus the mind that has full belief and faith in the results that will end up becoming a success story. The divine intervention is thus a way of saying that the Universe conspires with you to make you successful. The Universe sets in motion a number of coincidences and incidents to make sure you are a success.

Difficulty in life is to balance the religious theories versus with the modern knowledge of human mind's working. It is always a borderline subject and if you add on the location, language and culture to this mix we are looking at a kaleidoscope of colours, beliefs, and psyche. Indeed, the Indian psyche is multicultural in every possible way, filled with colours and multitude of beliefs within the same society. So at times, you will find that you are in a school or university where the teachers have a very different way of defining simple life principles. I wonder how a child copes with such opposite sets of theories in his mind thus trying to find a suitable one or a midway theory. If you try adding the complexity of the languages and dialects it might just be impossible to find a set of schools or Universities for our children to attend. Here is where I feel we can simplify the process of upbringing the child to making a perfect psyche lies in the simple principle of workings of the Universe. These principles are laid out in this chapter from the beginning to the end. I hope the reader will find the underlying meanings while reading between the lines to form his or her opinions.

Chapter One

Quo Vadis Indian Psyche?

Psyche is the Greek term meaning soul or spirit and it is widely used in psychology to define the totality of the human mind, conscious and unconscious thinking and action. In Roman and Greek mythology, Psyche, a beautiful girl loved by Cupid/Eros, who does the personification of the soul. The myth goes like this: Psyche was visited each night in the dark by Eros, who told her that she must not try to see him. When she did try, while he was asleep, she accidentally dropped the oil from her lamp on him and he awoke and fled. After she had performed many uphill tasks set by Cupid's mother, Venus, Jupiter made her immortal, and she and Eros were married. It is popularly used by psychoanalytic psychologists to denote the mental or psychological structure of a person, especially as a motivating force.

How to understand the Indian Psyche? It is a very simple question but it is not all that easy to answer. But there are subtle ways through which we can easily understand. Take the newspaper, read some news items that create some controversy among people or take a general problem in the society, and the way citizens, thinkers, leaders, decision makers and lawmakers reflect and react, clearly depict the psyche of the society.

Art and culture are some of the highly acclaimed participative, dynamic and social forms of human behaviour. Although the paucity of archaeological evidence limits our search for the origin and evolution of art in defining the uniqueness of human culture, art is one of the fundamental characteristics of the human species. By understanding art and culture in a society, we can easily understand human behaviour in a better way. Similarly, gender issues. Gender is how human beings perceive the self, based on life experiences, roles people play in homes, communities and society. Biology also shapes the source and foundation of socio-cultural elements which reflect the gender roles thus giving identity to human beings.

A lot of disturbing news headlines flash in the media today about people, socio-political groups and extremist and fundamental religious outfits trying to change the traditional culture of India, in the name of safeguarding tradition and faith. In extreme situations, the basic rights of the people are denied. When reflecting further, the incidents, reactions, reveal the present day Indian psyche. Let me invite the readers to a few moments of objective reflection, not based on emotions but using the intellect and reason.

Ramya Sedition Case: Kannada actress and politician Ramya[5], who visited Pakistan to for SAARC[6] meeting of young parliamentarians, spoke about the hospitality she received in Pakistan, how she felt, and how the people of Pakistan went out of their way to make her stay comfortable on getting to know she was from India.

- Lawyer files sedition case against Kannada Actor-politician Ramya: crime committed? She said 'Pakistan is Not Hell', after returning from Pakistan, where she had gone for the SAARC Young Parliamentarians Conference (Hindustan Times, August 23, 2016).

- Eggs were hurled at actress-turned-politician Ramya's car during a protest by BJP's youth wing in Mangaluru against her 'Pakistan is not hell' remark. Black flags were shown to the former MP as she came out of the airport by BJP Yuva Morcha activists who shouted

---

[5]Ramya born as Divya Spandana is a movie actress who mainly acts in Kannada and South Indian films. She entered politics in 2011 by joining the Indian Youth Congress and became a member of parliament in 2013 from Mandya constituency in Karnataka.

[6]SAARC - South Asian Association for Regional Cooperation was founded in Dhaka in 1985. It is a geopolitical, intergovernmental organization in South Asia with members from Afghanistan, Bangladesh, Bhutan, India, Nepal, the Maldives, Pakistan and Sri Lanka. Its headquarters is in Kathmandu.

"down down Ramya" and "Ramya go back" slogans (Deccan Chronicle, August 25, 2016).

Ramya is being trolled for her 'Pakistan is not hell' remarks. Outraged by her remarks, praising the people of Pakistan for their hospitality, a sedition complaint has been registered, a civil case under IPC sections 124 (A) 344 & 511 (sedition, wrongful confinement for ten or more days and punishment for attempting to commit offences punishable with imprisonment for life or other imprisonment) in magistrate's court in Karnataka's Kodagu district.

What is sedition act? In law, a sedition is an act such as speech or organization that tends toward rebellion against the established order. Section 124A of the Indian Penal Code states: whoever, by words, either spoken or written, or by signs, or by visible representation, or otherwise, brings or attempts to bring into hatred or contempt, or excites or attempts to excite disaffection towards, the Government established by law shall be punished with [imprisonment for life], to which fine may be added, or with imprisonment which may extend to three years, to which fine may be added. According to sedition act, a person can be punished only in situations where words and speech are being used to incite mobs or crowds to violent action. Mere words and phrases by themselves, no matter how distasteful, do not amount to a criminal offence unless this condition is met. However for the self-proclaimed 'nationalists' anything said in praise of another country itself is sedition. Sedition law is often misused by the self-styled extreme, hardcore nationalist groups, politicians, powerful people and anti-socials and the law needs to be clarified thoroughly. According to the lawyer who filed the case against Ramya, "she had insulted Indian patriots by praising Pakistan". This is absurd; the weird psyche thinks 'how dare a lady (from a political party that does not belong to nationalistic ideology) appreciate Pakistan which is India's arch rival?'. Probably in the course time this obsessive compulsive xenophobic patriotic lawyer who filed a case against Ramya may be worshipped and adored as a hero for taking it upon himself to save India from anyone saying good things about Pakistan; also his statues may be erected in the middle of the road junctions (to disturb the traffic) by the fanatic psychic outfits.

The words of Ramya were seen and observed in the backdrop of Defence Minister Manohar Parrikar's comments, who recently said that "going to Pakistan is the same as going to hell". One courageous politician reacted in this way: "those who believe that Pakistan is actually heaven should take next available flight to be warmly welcomed by terrorists, rapists & mullahs". I remember a sensible news reporter writes, "How does Ramya's remark qualify as an insult to India? Are we a psychologically insecure people with a serious inferiority complex whose ego gets offended by such harmless and mundane remarks? Are we turning into a typical jealous neighbour that begins to sulk every time somebody in the vicinity is praised?" (Sharma, 2016). However, such comments were not accepted by people who still think that Ramya is wrong.

Is this the Indian Psyche today? Are we affected by **xenophobia?**

Xenophobia is an unreasonable fear a person has or contemptuous of that which is perceived to be foreign or strange, especially of people from different countries or cultures. It can also be exhibited in many forms, ranging from mere love for one's own culture to hatred, communal violence and killing of people and eradication of another culture etc. The earliest example of xenophobia among Greek people is the condemnation of foreigners as barbarians and the general thought of Greek culture that they were superior to those of others. According to sociologists, racism, prejudice, cultural stereotypes and xenophobia are rampant in India today. It's an eccentric mixture of prejudice, ignorance and centuries-old discriminatory practices that different communities kept to themselves in India that is reflected among Indian psyche today.

As a reasonable netizen laments, 'Ramya didn't glorify Pakistan. She just said people like us live there, so calling Pakistan hell is improper. That's not glorification ... Pakistan state is evil, that they are bleeding India for decades. But that's a political, diplomatic, military issue ... We should be sober, graceful and dignified in dealing with Pakistan'. Only a few reasonable netizens give similar observations and they put their life under threat.

Dadri Lynching: Yet another shocking news report that gives a blow to our highly glorified tolerant culture and broad-mindedness came in the papers in the month of September 2015 as follows:

> A fifty-year-old Muslim man Akhlaq was beaten to death and his 22- year-old son was critically injured in a bizarre incident at Bisada village near Dadri, Uttar Pradesh, by a mob of about 100 people alleging that the family ate beef in the house. Police said they have sent samples of meat taken from Akhlaq's home "to the forensics department for examination". Akhlaq's daughter, Sajida, said the family had "mutton in the fridge" and not beef. The Indian Express reported that the incident took place on Monday night at around 10, 28 September 2015 in Dadri village, North Western Uttar Pradesh (UP), around 45 km from New Delhi (The Hindu, The Indian Express, September 30, 2015).

The story goes like this: on 28 September 2015 evening, two young lads announced in the local temple's public speaker that the family of Mohammad Akhlaq had killed a cow and consumed. On hearing this, a Hindu mob carrying sticks arrived at Mohammad Akhlaq's house within half-an-hour. Akhlaq and his son Danish were asleep and the other family members were about to go to sleep. The mob accused them of consuming beef and found some meat in the refrigerator. The family insisted that it was goat meat; however, the mob was not ready to listen to the story. They dragged the entire family outside and were attacked and abused physically. The neighbours tried to stop the mob but were not able to control the mob. The police were called and they arrived an hour later. By the time police arrived, Akhlaq was dead and Danish was badly injured.

The police arrested the temple's priest and his assistant for questioning. The temple priest denied any involvement in the incident and said that he was forced to make the announcement by some youngsters. The priest said that he had only announced that a cow had been killed and asked people to gather near the temple. FIR was filed against some of the attackers based on the report of Akhlaq's family. Later on, the number of arrests went up to eight. The arrests were protested by some local outfits and they started to protest against the arrest of murderers. The mob set fire to vehicles and vandalised shops. Some female relatives of the arrested persons attacked journalists and pelted stones at media vans. They claimed that these persons had been wrongly arrested and the media was covering only the victim's story. On June 9, 2016, judicial magistrate Vijay Kumar at the Surajpur district court issued a direction under section 156 (3), on a petition filed by a Bisara resident against murdered Mohammad Ikhlaq and his kin for alleged cow slaughter (Indian Express, July 15, 2016).

The cow has been a symbol of wealth in India since ancient times. However, they were not revered or kept in high esteem in the same way some people do today. In the Vedic period, cows were frequently slaughtered, both for consumption and in sacrifices. A legendary incident narrated in Tamil Literature Periapuranam[7] that happened in the life of a Chola king who is known as Manu Needhi Cholan (because of the magnificent steps he took to provide justice) who killed his own son in order to provide justice to a cow is noteworthy.

> One day the King's son while riding the chariot on the main roads of the capital city Thiruvarur and a calf suddenly entered in the road and was got hit by the wheel of the chariot and died. The cow which saw its calf killed on the street was stricken with grief. It licked the calf, cried and sat in grief near the dead calf. The king hung a huge bell in front of his palace courtroom for people to ring if they need justice from the king. The cow came to the palace and rang the bell seeking justice for the killed calf. Upon inquiry, a minister told the king that the calf entered beneath the chariot abruptly and got killed. Unable to bear the sight of the crying cow the King sat there in sadness and pondered what he could do to for the misdeed of his son. In order to provide justice to the cow, the King killed his own son in the same manner that the calf had been killed.

---

[7] Periyapuranam is a Tamil poetic collection by Sekkizhar during the rule of Kullottonga Chola II (1133-1150) which narrates the renowned lives of the sixty-three Nayanmars, the holy men of Tamil Shaivism.

A similar story is also popular in Srilanka, attributed to Chola King Ellalan. A 14th century stone temple in Lepakshi in Karnataka-Andhra border has a painting in the Natya Mandapa that depicts the story of Manu Needhi Cholan. A long panel, measuring nearly 40 square metres, narrates the story of Manu Needhi Cholan and the legendary event that took place at Thiruvarur. A more mythical version is seen in the art form in the temple in which it is pictured that the extraordinary justice was witnessed by various celestial bodies. Shiva and Parvati who witnessed it and came down to earth to restore the life of the prince and the calf and to give their blessing to the righteous king. I wonder whether the mythical story of Manu Needhi Cholan is created to propagate the significance of cow; there are kings who used titles such as Gobrahamana Pratipalanacharya (protector of cows and Brahmins).

Killing a cow is taboo in the majority of the states in India. Currently, 24 states have various regulations prohibiting either the slaughter or sale of cows. Kerala, West Bengal, Arunachal Pradesh, Mizoram, Meghalaya, Nagaland, Tripura, and Sikkim are the states where there are no restrictions on cow slaughter. India produced 3.643 million metric tons of beef in 2012, of which 1.963 million metric tons was consumed domestically and 1.680 million metric tons was exported. India ranks 5th in the world in beef production, 7th in domestic consumption and 1st in exporting (USDA, 2016).

India is a multireligious country and the culture of the people varies from place to place and also their food habits. About 80 % of the Indian population, comprising of Dalits, Adivasis, OBCs, Muslims and Christians etc eat beef. Eating beef has become a politically contentious issue in India in the past few years. Many states enacted laws which prohibit people possessing and eating beef a criminal act, even the Muslim inhabited Jammu and Kashmir state has banned beef. Some political parties use religious ideology as a means of getting votes and come to power. In such scenario, they try to be self-proclaimed cultural guardians of Indian tradition with a fascist ideology. The core ideology of some political parties and their off-shoots that champion caste hierarchy and harbouring ambitions to turn the secular India into a Hindu theocratic Rashtra is against the constitution of India.

On 13 September 2016, a religious leader announced that 'Muslims should refrain from eating beef for the sake of communal harmony. All people opposing a ban on cow-slaughter are satanic, fundamentalists and pseudo-secular'. A minister had asked all those who want to eat beef can 'go to Pakistan'. One religious leader had commented that the tragic earthquake of Nepal in April 2015 was caused by the sin of beef eating. Grownup people talking like children, probably this is what Sigmund Freud called *infantile neurosis*.

A legitimate question that is often raised by rational people would be: how come a leader of a particular religion advise people in a secular country to change their culture or tell what one has to wear or eat?

When we abuse people of another culture in the name of customs, practices and religion we are damaging the social fabric of Indian society as a whole. It is time to think: are Indians becoming intolerant or is it the original violent personality that is inherent in the psyche that is peeping out when political support is felt? If people continue this ideological and cultural obsession, India will be a laughing stock around the world.

Jain Monk Sermon Controversy: Haryana education minister Rambilas Sharma did a good job. He invited a Jain monk Tarun Sagar[8] to address the Haryana assembly. The Jain monk is a Digambara[9], (who was completely nude as per his religious customs), spoke about various issues and gave his own unscientific solutions in the 40 minutes sermon. His views received mixed comments from various sectors. Some comments are mild, some moderate and critical. Some

---

[8]Tarun Sagar, often called Muni, is a renowned Jain monk known for his critical sermons, called Kadve Pravachan (bitter discourses) dealing with family, social and political issues.

[9]Digambara and Shvetambara are the two major sects of Jainism. The word Digambara (Sanskrit) means sky clad and the other white-clad. Digambara monks do not wear any clothes. Nudity is one of the major doctrinal differences between the Shvetambaras and the Digambaras. The Digambara view on ascetic nakedness was put by Aparajita in the eighth century. The monk must follow the example of the Jinas, who were naked. However, nuns are allowed to be clothed as otherwise, they would cause social disruption.

felt, inviting religious leaders to address the legislative assembly itself reflects the rise of religiopolitical hegemony that is rising today in the secular Indian system. The Jain monk's views on religion and politics and the example of husband and wife raised alarms as if he is propagating sexism and misogyny.

Some positive suggestions by the monk: Politicians having criminal cases (those 160 MPs against whom cases have been registered) should not be allowed to climb the stairs of Lok Sabha and Vidhan Sabha. The proposed retirement age for politicians should be followed.

Some less attractive part of his sermon: Those who do not have daughters should not have the right to contest Lok Sabha and Vidhan Sabha elections. People should not marry their daughters into families that do not have daughters. Saints should not accept alms from houses where there are no daughters.

More controversial preaching: The control of dharma over politics is essential. Dharma is the husband, politics is the wife. It is the duty of every husband to protect his wife. It is the duty of every wife to accept the discipline of her husband. If there is no control of dharma over politics, it will be like an elephant out of control.

Vishal Dadlani[10], who was upset over the whole issue tweeted, 'People actually trying to defend the colossal idiocy of some naked monk, addressing the assembly, telling women how to live! unreal! ...That dude has the same education, as he has clothes on. None. I've no problem with nudity. I have a problem with religion in governance... If you voted for these people, you are responsible for this absurd nonsense'. The response of the singer is normal, yet his harsh words are slightly commentable. The reaction of some people on Dadlani's tweet was all the more ridiculous.

---

[10]Vishal Dadlani (1973) is a musician and vocalist and the lead artist in an original Indian independent music band, Pentagram (a rock/electronica band) started in 1994 in Mumbai, which has received recognition locally as well as globally. It is a four piece band: Vishal Dadlani – Vocals, Randolph Correia – Guitars, Papal Mane – Bass & Shiraz Bhattacharya – Drums.

- At least 27 people filed police complaints against an artist Dadlani for his tweets against the Jain monk in the assembly (Daily Mail, August 28, 2016)

- Vishal Dadlani's sarcastic tweet on Jain monk Tarun Sagar backfires, musician vows to quit politics (India Today, August 28, 2016)

- Under fire for tweet on Jain monk, Vishal Dadlani severs ties with Aam Aadmi Party (The Indian Express, August 29, 2016)

- After Twitter outrage, Vishal Dadlani apologizes for 33 times for targeting a Jain monk (Deccan Chronicle, August 28, 2016).

- Jain monk Tarun Sagar 'forgives' Vishal Dadlani for the irreverent tweet. (the Indian Express, August 29, 2016)

Punit Arora, a follower of the monk alleged that Dadlani had intentionally hurt religious sentiments with his sarcastic tweet. A case was filed against him under various sections of Indian Penal Code, including 153A (promoting enmity between classes) and 295A (maliciously insulting religion or religious beliefs). In a later development, when Dadlani approached the Supreme Court for anticipatory bail, the Supreme Court refused to protect Dadlani from arrest for his scathing remarks. Instead, the Supreme Court asked Dadlani's counsel to approach the High Court concerned to quash a FIR registered against him in Haryana. The counsel of Dadlani sought the court's protection from arrest at least till they apply to the High Court. But the court refused to budge. The Punjab and Haryana HC on Tuesday asked the Haryana government to show cause why the FIR against music composer Vishal Dadlani should not be quashed in its entirety.

However, Dadlani visited the Jain monastery of Muni Tarun Sagar and met him personally and asked forgiveness and blessings latter.

One Part Woman: Tiruchengode, a small town in Tamil Nadu became a centre of controversy when some communal outfits protested against Perumal Murugan for his novel *Madhorubagan*. Perumal Murugan is a professor of Tamil who has specialised in Kongu folklore. He has worked on building a lexicon of words, idioms, and phrases special to Kongu Nadu[11]. The moral police and the modern day cultural guardians of India made me read Perumal Murugan's *Madhorubagan*, translated into English by Aniruddh Vasudevan as *One Part Woman.*

When I was a little boy, way back in 1970's, I enjoyed reading a lot of Sandilyan's[12] historical fictions that were published as serial stories in Kumudam magazine. *Kadal Pura, Raja Muthrai, Raja Perigai* etc.. etc are my favourites. Prince travelling in a horse, meeting a beautiful girl in a fountain, or taking a long voyage, meeting his lady love in secret are real fest to my reading pleasure. During my college days, I became Leo Tolstoy's[13] fan and loved *Resurrection, War and Peace, Anna Karenina* and *Father Sergius.* Leo Tolstoy was very cruel with the monk Sergius!!!

The novel I read recently was a Sahitya Akademi[14] award-winning novel *Thoopukari*; that too, because I know the author personally. I

---

[11]Kongu Nadu is a region comprises of the western Tamil Nadu and parts of the states of Karnataka & Kerala. The region was ruled by the Cheras during Sangam period and latter by many Tamil Kingdoms. An archaeological finding from Kodumanal, on the banks of the River Noyyal, suggests that there was an ancient unique culture existed here from 4th century BCE.

[12]Sandilyan or Chandilyan (1910-1987) is the Penname of Bhashyam Iyengar, a popular Tamil writer, known for his historical romance and adventure novels, often set in the times of the Chola and Pandiya Empires. He was educated at St. Joseph's College, Tiruchirapalli. His historical novels were published in book form by Vanadhi Padhippagam and became best sellers. According to a netizen Raja Gopalan, many of Sandilyan's novels are plagiarized from Rafael Sabatini's (an Italian-English writer of novels of romance and adventure) works. For example, Jeeva Bhoomi, based in Rajputana originates from Sabatini's Bardelys the Magnificent; the sea battles in Kadalpura are from Captain Blood; Yavana Rani comes from The Sea Hawk, all in Indian historical figures.

[13]Leo Tolstoy (1828-1910) was one of the greatest Russian writers. He is best known for his works War and Peace (1869) and Anna Karenina (1877). His novel Resurrection (1899) depicts his economic philosophy which he himself adopted in his writing and also in real life. The novel highlights the injustice of man-made laws and the duplicity of the institutionalized Christianity.

[14]The Sahitya Akademi in India is a National Academy of Letters, dedicated to the promotion of literature in Indian languages founded on 12 March 1954.

was curious to know whether anything known to me about the author is reflected in her novel[15].

Mathorupagan is a disturbing story of a childless couple and the pathological fixation to have a child. The novel ends with a ritualistic practice in Tiruchengode a century ago, which permits childless women to go with any man on the night of the festival and the child born out of such a secret, the unknown union was treated as a gift of God; a customary sexual permissiveness is narrated in the novel. Perumal Murugan talks about a cultural practice, probably an ancient cultural solution, like the one *Niyoga*, an orthodox praxis now sounds unorthodox.

Niyoga (Niyog pratha) is an ancient tradition wherein a widowed woman or the wife of a man incapable of fathering any children can request a male relative of the husband, usually the brother, to help her bear a child. Though there are various debates and oppositions regarding the tradition, it was quite a prevalent practice in ancient India, mentioned in The Mahabharata, The Vedas, The Ramayana and many other writings. Niyoga practices have changed or evolved from the times of Sacred Scriptures to the modern times, to suit the requirements of society at various time periods in history. The concept of Niyoga is not solely an Indian concept or tradition; it has also seen in other cultures like Israel and in many African cultures too. Warsa practice, for example in Northern Ethiopia, is a similar tradition practised even today. Although education and awareness programs have reduced the usage of this custom to a greater extent, it is still a customary practice among uneducated rural population in Ethiopia.

Most likely, the sexual liberalism reported in the book of Professor Perumal Murugan is a kind of artificial insemination in which a man was allowed to impregnate a woman on anonymous conditions. This is what Perumal Murugan wrote in his novel.

---

[15] Thoopukari is a Sahitya Akademi award winning novel written by Malarvathi (Mary Flora) from a small village Vellikodu on the side of Kannya Kumari-Trivandrum Highway. Thoopukari is a term used to call a woman sanitary worker in Kanyakumari area and the novel depicts the anxiety and pain of a girl whose mother is a sanitary worker.

Devadasi system is a religious practice in southern India whereby parents marry a daughter to a deity or a temple, usually before the girl attains puberty. The girl becomes a prostitute for upper-caste community members. They are forbidden to enter into a real marriage. Originally, the devadasis had a high status in society. After marrying a wealthy patron, they spent their time honing their skills instead of becoming a housewife. Their children were also taught the skills of music or dance. Often their patrons had different wives who served them as housewives.

There are also conflicting reports on the history and development of devadasis and temple prostitution tradition. According to some historians, after the fall of Buddhism, when their temples were taken over by the Brahmins, the Buddhist nuns were made temple prostitutes. Some authors suggest, when the temples became poorer or lost their patron kings and destroyed, the temple dancers were forced into poverty and prostitution. According to some hypothesis, it is a great conspiracy between the high-class feudal heads and the Brahmin priests to hold their superiority devised a religious way to exploit lower caste people introduced prostitution. The devadasi system has been outlawed all of India since 1988 and today no sensible person will approve such practice. Does that mean, if someone writes a novel based on that s/he degrades our culture? Sati was a funeral ritual practiced in ancient India. Nobody approves such practice today. Can we oppose someone who writes a novel based on that?

Indian psyche has lost its glorious tolerance and the golden lotus of Buddha is clouded by the present day socio-politico-religious jingoism. A narrow-minded fanaticism has become the symbol of Indian Psyche, overshadowing tolerant, open minded past.

The image that India is a tolerant country was partly an imaginary concept that evolved from the various inversions from outside since time immemorial. It is also a legacy of the ideals of the recent non-violent independence movement and Nehru's non-alignment foreign policy. Indian spirituality and the philosophical and yogic traditions gave rise to this perception and image. However, this tolerant platonic outlook has been challenged by many fundamentalist sociopolitical and religiopolitical outfits today. Religious tolerance and communal harmony are testing Indian image globally. As Pethiyagoda (2015) points out, 'the current Government holds a large majority in parliament, implementing religion-based policies, politicians making incendiary comments, all the way down to grassroots activists running amok'.

Narrow mindedness in interpersonal dealings, backwardness in thinking, extreme selfishness in interpersonal relations, aggressive behaviour in public, cowardly attacks on minority groups for any perceived or imaginary disturbance, exploitation of poor by money power and political authority, corruption in every possible sector - both in government and non-government are norms of the day and has become the part and parcel of Indian culture today. Still, we trumpet our past glory and raise slogans that ours is the great country; *'if you don't agree you are a condemned criminal'*. As cultural, moral and religious vigilantism is strongly creeping into the daily culture of the people, religious freedom is on a negative trajectory. Is it the slow death of tolerant culture in India or the *maya* of tolerance is slowly vanishing as the reality of aggressive fundamentalism emerging?

Chapter Two

Sex Taboos in India[16]

The worldview of the rural Indian psyche still continues to hold the remnants of the chronological ideologies of sex norms, mores, and taboos in such an ambiguous way as they look at sex as sensual. The relics and glimpses of historical ideological bases cause an enormous amount of guilt and shame in the minds of the rural community, thus regulating their moral activities. A widening gap between sex norms and sexual behaviour is seen in the social transit from traditional sacredness to modern sensualism. Education, urban migration, mass media, government legislations and pressure groups contribute to the current sex concept, norms, and taboos. As a result, some sex taboos are abandoned and new taboos emerge. The study identifies the current worldview that Sex is Sensual emerges at the backdrop of traditional Indian philosophical concept Sex is Sacred, Islamic ideology Sex is Secret and the colonial dogma Sex is Sin and Shame. The current worldview also reflects the various historical timeframes, major political occupations and religious influences the Indian subcontinent has undergone.

Over the millennia, rural communities have developed and sustained practical social norms and systems to safeguard their wellbeing. The evidence clearly correlates that socio-cultural norms and practices provide social support and enhanced coping mechanisms for people

---

[16]Co-authored by **Mini TC** & **Ravishankar** and presented in the 8th Biennial Conference of Asian Association of Social Psychology, IIT, Delhi.

during difficult times. However, due to modern globalization, amplified mass media, alluring urban life and migration for better jobs and education, the serene rural lifestyle is undergoing a major overhaul and traditional social norms have been increasingly displaced. Rural communities face somewhat turbulent state in most regions of the world due to these emerging conditions. This obtains true in the Indian rural communities too.

Human sexuality is a multifarious topic in India today. In the ancient Indian community, more than anywhere else in the world, sex was a matter of talk, study and research. It was this open and sundry attitude of the ancient Indian society that gave the Kamasutra[17] to the world. Sex was sacred and, sexual union was considered a medium by which couples enter sex and procreate. The worship of lingam and yoni and architectural display of sexual acts on the walls of temples and places of worship depict the picture of the tale of a different sexual culture. Therefore the concept of human sexuality today in India is a complex praxis that has passed through several stages of contrasting ideology and concepts.

The word taboo often referred to any a social or religious custom prohibiting or restricting a particular practice or forbidding association with a particular person, place, or thing. Breaking such taboo was considered objectionable or abhorrent by society. The word taboo became popular in the psychological circles after the best known anthropological magnum work of Sigmund Freud Totem and Taboo in which Sigmund Freud provides an insightful description of many

---

[17]Kāma means desire which includes sexual desire and sūtra literally means a thread or line that holds things together, and more metaphorically refers to an aphorism or a collection of such aphorisms in the form of a manual. The Kama Sutra is an ancient Indian Hindu manuscript written by Vātsyāyana, often considered to be the standard work on human sexual behaviour in Indian literature. Contrary to the Western observation that the Kama Sutra is an exclusive sex manual, it is a guide to a virtuous and gracious living that discusses the nature of love, family life and other aspects pertaining to pleasure oriented faculties of human life. Only a portion of the work talks about practical advice on sexual intercourse. The majority of the book is about the philosophy and theory of love, what triggers desire, what sustains it, how and when it is good or bad.

taboos and their origination (1905)[18]. Today taboos have got a broader connotation indicating many of the forbidden human social behaviours that regulate nearly every realm of our life, sexual conduct, caste relations, social institutions, and socio-political mechanisms.

In the primitive as well as modern communities, sex taboos are prominently seen in serious issues like incest, rape, paraphilias, and marriage regulations to small discussions regarding sex-related behaviours. Today there is an emerging trend and penchant for sex. A clear mitigation is seen from the traditional conservative concept which is evident from the fact that sex is liberally plastered on billboards, broadcast on televisions, heard everywhere in the lyrics of favourite songs, themes, and scenes in movies, magazines, newspapers and on the internet and mobile handsets. At the same time, some elements of conservatism are also seen and heard in different circles. Although the urban proclivity for liberal sex has not penetrated the rural communities fully, openness to education and urban life are an unavoidable necessity that easily initiates rural communities to the liberal trends and more so the transient rural population to the practices of the dominant adjacent urban culture. The emergence of new concepts, worldview, and different praxis place the rural communities in a predicament in which the younger generation is confused due to the fact that on the one hand the elders propagate one socio-cultural value and on the other the society is practising different social behaviour. In this background, this research was focused on the current scenario of the Indian rural communities regarding sex concepts and taboos and the role of different factors that contribute to

---

[18]Freud was one of the early psychologists who made a thorough examination of myths in religion, using his own understanding of human mind in his book Totem and Taboo in 1912-13. The book proposes that all contemporary socializations are formed by primitive culture and societies. Also, he states that all forms of conformity behaviours spring from a common primitive form. He also talks about how modern and monotheistic religions came into being. His theories have been heavily criticized, and have been a source of major controversies since they were first put forward. Freud's own drastic explanation to the birth of religion could be seen in Moses and Monotheism, which was not very scientific, has mostly met with rejection from theologians and historians of religion, was published in 1939.

the nature of conformity, obedience to traditional culture and also for the emerging deviance. Knowing the taboos in the communities will help social scientists and other scholars to evaluate the stands of rural communities to know their attitude and behaviour better. Knowing the current condition of the rural communities would help people to have cultural empathy and develop sensitivity towards rural communities. Evaluating the taboos can also help determine the root of the dysfunction, psychosocial as well as psychosexual dynamisms and causes of mental health issues and disorders. This in return will aid clinicians to have better knowledge on diagnostic criteria as DSM-IV[19] and other diagnostic manuals emphasize the necessity to take into account the individual's cultural context regarding each of the diagnostic praxes.

Indian Rural Community: The word community refers to a collection of people with similar identity, influence, integration and fulfilment of needs and, share the emotional connection (McMillan & Chavis, 1986). The German sociologist Tonnies (1957) defines community as associations that are intimate, familiar, sympathetic, mutually interdependent, and reflective of a shared social consciousness. Generally, the common characteristics identified with the community are proximity, geographical as well as human relationships, common values and beliefs, strong group feeling and cultural similarity. In the Indian rural community, a strict control over the individual and their actions are employed by caste and creed norms, elders in the family, whether it is joint family or nucleus, and the governing local panchayat.

---

[19] DSM-IV (a publication of American Psychiatric Association) is a collection of all recognized mental health to help identify which features make up a certain disorder and how to distinguish it from the others. The coding system of DSM corresponds to the ICD (published by UN) in such a way that it complements and gives additional information that would not be part of ICD. Both give importance to the cultural content of psychiatric diagnosis and well-recognized cultural variables, adequate family data, and strengs and weaknesses of every individual patient.

Caste[20] is a vital unifying force in Indian rural communities (Ghurye, 1961). Caste refers to a hereditary group inherited by the virtue of birth and extended by endogamous marriages. Some caste and communities have a specific traditional occupation to earn their livelihood. It is more than occupation and profession, the unique distinct culture and customs that distinguish one caste from another. Mainly they are reflected in behavioural patterns, food habits, taboos and totems prescribed by the tradition.

Social Norms and Deviance: Morris Ginsberg (2003) defines society as a collection of individuals united by certain relations and mode of behaviours which identify them different from others. Open societies easily accept change and new ideas whereas closed ones resist change. Social norms consist of rules of conduct and models of behaviour prescribed by a society rooted in the customs, traditions and value systems. There is a difference between social norms and actual social behaviour. Social norms emerge from social values and passed through symbolic communication in the communities (Ortega, 1957). Norms are the means through which values are expressed in the society often accepted or imposed and passed on from generation to generation. When people in a community turn away from the existing social norms it is deviance. Deviance, therefore, consists of those areas which do not follow the norms and expectations of a particular social group with the certain level of tolerance and acceptance because deviance varies from time to time and place to place. Frank Elwell (2006) citing Durkheim argues social changes begin with deviance. A deviant behaviour in one society is followed as normal behaviour in

---

[20]Caste is a form of social stratification characterized by endogamy, transmission of occupation and exclusion based on cultural notions of purity and pollution, sometimes leading the society into rigid social groups. Today, it is a curse in the Indian society in which fundamental groups from higher caste treat the lower levels as untouchables. At the same time, in the Indian politics, this division is used to lure specific caste groups for getting votes. In the intellectual and professional level, by perpetuating a caste and creed based job selection policies (reservation and quota system policies for different castes at various levels), many lower and higher intellectual and decision-making bodies are filled with un-performing and underperforming candidates and thus creating a brain-drain in the society by not selecting the right person based on aptitude and talent.

another society and, people mingle or open to various societies often show deviant behaviours. In a more conservative society, a deviant behaviour is punished by sanctions and isolations.

Social Change and Disorganization: Auguste Comte[21] (1856) the French philosopher and founder of sociological positivism believed that social change is a progress toward something better and positively beneficial. This concept was supported by Herbert Spencer[22]. This view is highly influenced by Charles Darwin's theory of Evolution. There are sociologists who argue that social changes in communities are like a cycle that revolve growth and decay (Spengler 1991, Toynbee, 1946 & Sorokin, 1938). Parsons (1951) however looks cultural patterns as something that does not disturb the social equilibrium either they come from outside the society from inside the society, they control the stability of a society. There are also sociologists who suggest that social disorganization is an inevitable reality of any society in the course of time, as part of change. Conflict is a normal process and continuous conflict keeps society dynamic and ever changing (Dahrendorf, 1959). It, however, destabilizes the harmonious running of various parts of culture. Therefore, social organization and social disorganization are the two sides of any society. Modern sociologists consider disorganization among institutions as a normal process by which institutions are rationally adapted to changing conditions as well as a normal consequence of social change (Bursik, 1984). According to Maciver and Page (1962), social change is a complex phenomenon that involves many factors like psychological, biological, physical, technological and cultural.

---

[21]Auguste Comte (1798-1857) is a French philosopher who was born between the time of the French Revolution and modern science and technology. Comte spent much of his life developing a philosophy for a new social order amidst all the chaos and uncertainty in many parts of Europe.

[22]Herbert Spencer (1820-1903) was a British philosopher, sociologist and one of the principal proponents of evolutionary theory in the mid-nineteenth century. Spencer was best known for developing and applying evolutionary theory to philosophy, psychology and the study of society often referred to as 'synthetic philosophy'. Today, however, he is usually remembered in philosophical circles for his political and social thoughts.

When these factors bring out changes in the social structure, the chaos can no longer able to be controlled by the society and their social disorganization crop up. Sorokin (1970) is of the opinion that disorganization is mainly due to cultural degeneration of values in various spheres such as art, science, philosophy, religion, law and politics.

Worldview: Worldview is comprehensive conception or apprehension of the world especially from a specific standpoint. Worldview affects how one views different aspects of life - physical, emotional, spiritual, moral, sociological and mental. It is reflected in and through culture. As Gordon (1978) points out, culture represents the way of life and thinking of groups in a society, and it consists of prescribed ways of behaving and doing, norms of conduct, beliefs and value systems. These customary behaviours are oftentimes protected and preserved to enable the communities to maintain their identity. Worldview is one's philosophy of life, mindset, outlook on life, a formula for life, ideology, faith, or even religion. It is neither a fixed reality nor fully comprehended and throughout history, we see evidence of emerging worldviews. New worldviews emerge not by replacing old worldview rather subsumes the preceding worldviews (Leith, 2003). This emergence is a perennial process often facilitated taboos and totems, psychosocial functioning, and expressions of distress.

Sex Concepts and Taboos: The word taboo was first introduced into English in 1777 by James Cook[23] after his second voyage to the Pacific Islands. The term originally used in the Tongan language, and appears in many Pacific Island cultures with specific religious associations (Marshall, 1998). A taboo is a strong social prohibition relating to any

---

[23]Captain James Cook (1728-1779) was a captain in the British Royal Navy known as an explorer, superior navigator with excellent surveying and cartographic skills and also physical courage and leadership qualities to lead men in adverse conditions. Cook sailed thousands of miles across the uncharted parts of the earth in his three voyages and gave a detailed map of Pacific Ocean, the coastline of Australia and the Hawaiian Islands, and the first recorded circumnavigation of New Zealand. He was attacked and killed in a confrontation with Hawaiians during his third exploratory voyage in the Pacific in 1779.

area of human activity or social custom that is sacred and forbidden. Freud (1913) conceptualized that cultural taboos of sexual morals and practices are the root cause of many neuroses among people. Although many people in the Western societies consider this concept of Freud outdated, it is a truism as far as Indian rural society is concerned. One of the supernatural causes of illness in the traditional community is a taboo violation (Torrey, 1986). A taboo violation occurs when a person behaves contrary to traditional teachings and customs. When sex taboos, sex mores, and daily practices change, communities struggle in crossroads due to the fusion of mixed cultural values. These confused states of mind highlight the transitional symptoms in the rural communities.

India played a significant role in the history of sex by giving the world the much acclaimed Kamasutra as well as the new-age sensual philosophy of Osho Rajneesh[24]. However, today rural communities lack healthy sex concepts and attitude. According to a 2006 Indian Health Bureau report, 78 percent of Indians below the age of 20 do not know about safe sex. The same report reveals that 54 percent adolescents are sexually active. A lot of teenagers are having sex without having proper knowledge about sex. The government initiative to introduce sex education in schools is a failure. In the words of former Health Minister Ramadoss, 'We are not taking up sex education in a blatant manner but in a subtle way... have 55% of our population that falls in the reproductive age, and we have to create awareness among them'. These views were not received positively and a majority of Indian states have banned or not introduced sex education. Although sex education is a taboo, liberalized and globalized younger generations are trending towards a more open, casual attitude towards sex both in rural and urban centres. Young

---

[24]Chandra Mohan Jain (1931-1990), known as Bhagwan Shree Rajneesh Osho was a mystic, guru, cult leader and spiritual teacher. He began his career as a professor of philosophy and started his own ashram at Pune to preach his way of living. He uses traditional Indian philosophy in a modern way and attracted many foreign and Indian followers to his way of meditation. He was a strong critic of institutionalised religions and advocated a more open attitude towards human sexuality, often referred to as 'sex guru'.

urbanites are more promiscuous and precarious than their counterparts.

The following data was collected from Idukki and Coimbatore districts in South India. Idukki is one among the 14 districts of Kerala state with an area of 5105.22 sq.km. The district borders the Kerala districts of Pathanamthitta to the south, Kottayam to the southwest, Ernakulam to the northwest and Thrissur to the north and Coimbatore, Dindigul and Theni Districts in Tamil Nadu to the east. The total population of Idukky district is 11,08,974 (2011 census). The district has a population density of 255 inhabitants per square kilometre. Malayalam and Tamil are the principal languages spoken in this district. Hindus form the majority of the population followed by Muslims, Christians, and tribal communities. The literacy rate of this district is 91.99%. Coimbatore district lies in the western part of Tamil Nadu, part of the Kongu Nadu region. The district borders with Kerala with Idukki in the south and Palakkad district in the west; it borders with Tamil Nadu in the north with Nilgiris, Erode in the north-east and east, and Dindigul district in the south-east. It has a population of 3,458,045 (2011 census) and a literacy rate of 83.98 %. Tamil is the principal language spoken in the district, with sizable minorities of Telugu, Malayalam and Kannada speakers. Hindus form the majority of the population at 90.08% followed by Muslims, Christians, and others.

Participants of this study composed of two groups a) 48 key informants – these subjects were believed to be the most credible, well-informed and most familiar with the place, people, and cultural practices. b) 420 secondary informants - participants from the general population of both the study districts. This includes students, workers, farmers and housewives of various age groups. This exploratory study used qualitative techniques to gather and analyze data. A mixture of ethnography and phenomenology methods, specifically, in-depth interview and focus group discussion and other indigenous methods were used to collect data.

Results and Discussion: The emerging worldview and sex concepts have to be understood in terms of the social milieu in which it exists. It is evidently inherent in the socio-cultural context with various contemporaneous influences that occur over a period of time. The study identifies three ideological bases that have been inculcated down through the centuries which constitute the core concept of sex in rural communities namely:

i) sex is sacred
ii) sex is secret
iii) sex is sin and shame

These bases owe its origin in the historical, political history India underwent at different times and the consequential paradigm shifts that have taken place, one bearing on the other and the change and impact continues till date.

When we go back to the days of yore, sex was construed in society as something sacred and had its own divine acceptance. The ancient Indian philosophical systems and the related religious conservation have established sex as an instrumental act of procreation and part of cosmic rhythm in its entirety. It is this notion of creative function, placed human sex in a symbolic way akin to God's creation. This social milieu in which sex was sacred and divine, marriage a divine sacrament underwent a sea of change due to Muslim invasion of India. The spiritual, divine furrow which was in the collective unconscious of the community gradually gave way to personal conscious level imprisoning sex to the veils of secrecy. Changes in gender roles, prohibitions in man-women social contact, expression of affection, mirroring women as an inferior creature and portraying her as an object of sex – all tell the tale that sex is to be confined to the inner walls of the house. These attuned socio-sexual norms, as they emerged, projected sex as an innately private affair and thus secret.

The influence of colonial rulers of Europe and British rule in specific ushered the Indian society to the Western Victorian mores with the Biblical mythical creation stories at the backdrop and dualistic theology of Judaism and Christianity, propagated norms and values with strong eschatological overtures that influenced the Indian society to imbibe the concept sex is sin and shame. These paradigm shifts at regular intervals, through different politico-religious backgrounds and setup in India, have not totally eliminated one or other earlier concept, rather just as any other socio-cultural praxis, sex taboos too were added or replaced in the course of time. In the fact, the three ideological bases mentioned above related to sex concepts and norms generated or eliminated sex taboos that are still in practice in varying modified degrees and forms. Added to that is the modern liberated morals of American society that is widespread due to mass media and multinational establishments all over India under the banner of globalization has emanated the concept sex is sensual. As Geetanjali Chanda (2001) points out, "The influx of foreign companies in the country brings more than just employment opportunities and economic benefits to the country. They bring with them a certain attitude and a mindset that promotes liberalism and, among other things, openness about sexuality".

This mixture of sacred, secret, sin and shame concept as well as the modern sensual dictum is commonly reflected in popular culture and movie themes of today. It is this sensual concept of sex today Kakar (1989) narrates, 'the cultural splitting of the wife into a mother and as well as a whore, contradictory Hindu views of the woman, is hardly unique to Indian culture, though it may be more pervasive here than in other cultures'. The modern sensual concept that has been depicted as a liberated concept is an added attraction to many even in the remotest rural

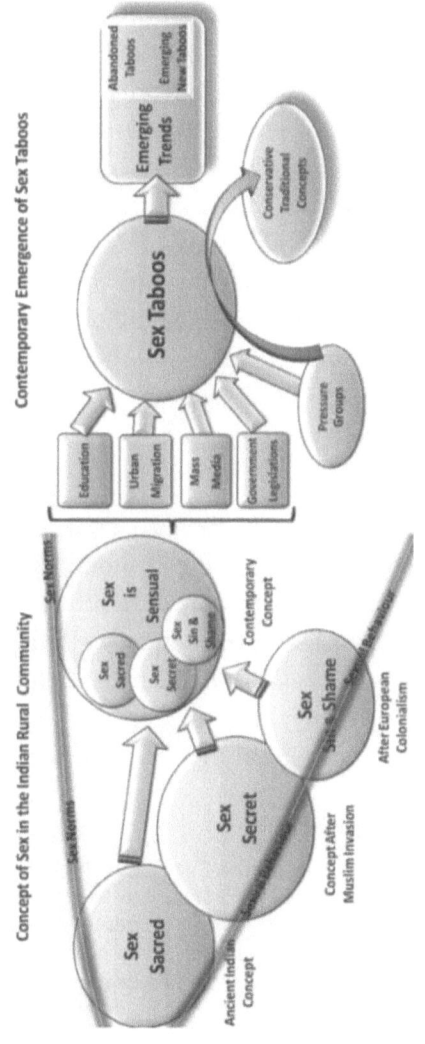

37

communities and the younger generation run berserk falsifying and dethroning many of the older taboos and norms.

Although sex is sensual, the relics of the historical concepts still gives an enormous amount of psychic pain and guilt feeling in the minds of rural population regulating their moral activities. Therefore it is a fact that in the current worldview and in the rural Indian psyche the glimpses of sex concepts and norms namely, sex is sacred, sex is secret, and sex is sin and shame, in such an ambiguous way as the communities look at sex as sensual. Inherently, the present day rural psyche of both young and old still appears to have a stronger grip on the traditional beliefs and concepts in spite of mass media and other outside influences. The inherited traditional belief is the product of a continuous genetic informational flow in reproduction which is identified by Freud as "archaic inheritance" and Carl Jung as "collective unconscious"[25].

This concept of inherent cultural values is further explained by a recent theory of Richard Dawkins, who coins the word *meme* in his book *The Selfish Gene*[26] to identify this phenomenon. Dawkins defines *meme* as a unit of intellectual or cultural information, which is metaphorically equivalent to the genes (Watson, 1995). Just as genes transmit biological genetic qualities from generation to generation, memes carry culture from generation to generation. They are passed on both vertically to the next generation and horizontally to others in

---

[25] Collective unconscious is a term coined by Carl Jung to refer the structures of unconscious mind which are shared among beings of the same species. Jung distinguishes it from the personal unconscious of Freudian psychoanalysis. Sigmund would call this 'archaic remnants', a kind of mental forms which seem to be aboriginal, innate, and inherited shapes of the human mind. Both talk about the same idea of an archaic ancestor maintaining its influence in the minds of present-day humans.

[26] Richard Dawkins (born 1941) is a British evolutionary biologist who is well known for his criticism of creationism. *The Selfish Gene* (1976) talks about the gene-centred view of evolution; he also uses the word meme for a unit of human cultural evolution analogous to the gene, suggesting that such selfish replication may also model human culture, in a different sense. He is an atheist and in his most popular book, *The God Delusion* (2006), he argues that religious faith is a delusion.

the community. The widening gap between social norms and social behaviour as the society transforms from conservative towards liberal are seen by the younger generation as progressive conversely by the older generation as deviance. This conservative–liberal dichotomous sexual concepts and the consequent behaviours have a profound impact in the social fabric which has resulted in developing a piquant socio-cultural situation where in social norms continue to persist with the old sex taboos taking an ideological frame, while the modern liberal social behaviour tends to deviate. Politico-religious pressure groups[27], as they surface at times are dismayed at the deviating socio-cultural sexual praxis, pressurize the society towards the maintenance of their status-quo, which is often conservative and traditionalistic. It is a social tug-of-war between the pressure groups and the modern society in which one group adversely forcing to narrow the gap between social norms and explicit behaviours whereas the other obviously widening the gap. However, some socio-politico pressure groups that emerge at situations force the society abandon currently meaningless sex norms and pave way for liberal attitude. The emerging contemporary sex concepts, taboos, and praxis in the rural communities are nothing but the ubiquitous social conflict that produces instability, struggle and social disorganization in bringing out social change as theorized by renowned social conflict proponents Ralf Dahrendorf, Karl Marx and Engel. The widening gap ranges from being latent in some communities and unambiguous in others.

Contemporary Emergence of Sex Taboos: There are five sociological determinants that given birth to the contemporary sex norms and taboos namely: a) education, b) mass media, c) urban-migration, d) government legislations, e) pressure groups. These five factors

---

[27]Pressure groups are collections of people with a parallel set of values and beliefs generally based on ethnicity, religion, political philosophy, or some common goal. Pressure groups are potentially beneficial to any democratic society, in which they pressurise the government for more action. In India, however, pressure groups with a narrow notion of nationalism and also a clubbing religion with nationalism by their political theory create communal tensions in India rather than giving democratic suggestions to the governments. Political parties often lure the pressure groups to perpetuate their power.

influence the current generation to abandon or cling to the remnants of their ancestors' traditional social norms and way of life. These, in consequence, push the current rural community to abandon some sex taboos as well as adopt new ones. The impact of mass media and government legislations and socio-political pressure groups has a direct bearing on abandoning certain taboos. Human being's quest for a meaningful existence is the highest aspiration and motivation today. This quest has spread wide in the field of religion, the scriptures too, which results in various exegeses of the scriptures in the West, especially the Bible. Can this quest be quenched fully? Can religious language become intelligible to modern human mind? It is a great challenge today.

A strong barrier and deterrent to the progression of social thinking and the emerging new taboos come from the impact of strong politico-religious pressure groups that emerge now and then that lead the society to preserve and safeguard fundamental concepts. A fine example of this fact is the modern nude sculptures of Kanai Kunjuraman[28] in Kerala. Around 50 years ago, one of his first major sculptures 'Yakshi' (nude 30-feet giant size) in Malampuzha Dam gardens in Palakkad, Kerala sculpted against the backdrop of the Western Ghats created controversy. During the time of creation, the artist was beaten up and the work was halted for nearly 3 months. Yakshi was condemned as obscene; a deviation from existing forms of sculptures because people are not accustomed to seeing nude statues outside the temples. The nude female vampire (yakshi) and a huge Nymph (Jalakanyaka) and similar artefacts that had to face stiff opposition from different pressure groups because nudity is not fully accepted by the people of Kerala and the nude female statues in the

---

[28]Kanayi Kunhiraman (born 1937) is a sculptor from Kasaragod district of Kerala State, India. He did some basic education in artworks from Fine Arts College, Chennai (1960) and Slade School of Art, London (1965). Kanayi Kunhiraman began erecting sculptures in public places and since then he has been living with controversies. Most of his artworks depict a unique amalgamation of heritage, myth, and folklore. Even after many controversies, he was the first sculptor recipient of the Raja Ravi Varma Award in 2005.

state were a matter of debate by these groups. Although King Ravi Varma[29] (1848-1906) one of the greatest painters in the history of Indian Arts has honestly painted nude arts in the same state a century ago, which was over and again acclaimed by the same population as pieces of acclaimed art, today a taboo has been framed due to pressure groups. Conversely, in Tamil Nadu Widow Remarriage taboo is abandoned due to socio-political pressure groups from the Dravidian movement started by E. V. Ramasamy[30] that has been made into government legislation. The abolishing old taboos are often hailed partly as progressive whereas in certain quarters of society condemned as the annihilation of traditional mores. The tables in the following pages show some of the emerging new taboos and the major contributing factors in the rural communities.

Abandoned and Emerging New Taboos: As the society moves into the new millennium, the sex concepts and norms have been redefined due to many factors. Education, government legislations, urban migration, mass media and the socio-politico pressure groups have contributed a lot to the abandoning of many sex taboos. The prominent abandoned taboos could be identified as inter-caste and inter-religious marriages,

---

[29]Raja Ravi Varma (1848-1906) was closely related to the royal family of Travancore in Kerala and was recognised as one among the greatest painters in the history of Indian art. His works are noted for the fusion of European techniques with an Indian sensibility. He painted few nude and semi-nude paintings of both women and apsaras like Urvashi, Rambha from Hindu mythology. He was also charged at Bombay court with cases of obscenity, offending public morality and hurting religious and cultural sentiments of people.

[30]Periyar E. V. Ramasamy (1879 -1973), also known as Thanthai Periyar was a Dravidian social reformer and politician from South India. He dealt harshly with caste discrimination and attacked those who used the system to take advantage. In 1952, Rajaji introduced a new education policy based on family vocation which its opponents dubbed Kula Kalvi Thittam (Hereditary Education Policy) in Tamil Nadu. Thus, a carpenter's son would learn carpentry, a priest's son chanting hymns, and a barber's son would learn hair cutting and shaving after school. Periyar demanded its withdrawal and launched protests against the Kula Kalvi Thittam which he felt was caste-based and was aimed at maintaining caste hegemony. Periyar encouraged inter-caste marriages and organised thousands of weddings between people of different communities and without the intervention of Brahmin priests.

family planning and having less number of children, widow remarriage, and puberty-related rituals and menstruation-related prohibitions. The inter-caste and inter-religious marriage was a taboo in the rural communities until recently and now has gone to the depths due to government legislation and urban migration. For years India has been divided and isolated themselves on the basis of caste and creed. The government of Tamil Nadu has initiated incentive packages for inter-caste marriages that removed the taboo attached to the practice. Similarly, widow remarriage was a taboo thrown out mainly by socio-politico pressure groups, education, and government legislations.

Emerging new Taboos	Major Contributing Factor
Nudity in art	Politico-Religious Pressure Groups
Semi-nakedness and new dress codes	Mass media
Polygamy	Education
Number of Children	Education, Urban Migration
Child marriage	Government Legislations, Education

In the same way, government legislations have eliminated the taboo of family planning in the rural communities. Having many children was a blessing and highly encouraged activity where family planning was an anathema. Other abandoned taboos are Puberty and menstruation-related taboos. Puberty taboos are popular rural customs in which the girl who attains puberty is isolated and specific rituals done at home. Similarly, menstruation taboos considered ladies unclean and thus forbid them from certain daily functions. However, these age-old popular practises are abandoned due to education and mass media. As far as the emerging new taboos are concerned, the politico-religious pressure groups play a vital role in pressurizing the community for more conservative traditional concepts. Education and government legislations have eradicated some social evils by creating some taboos in the society, for example, child marriage and polygamy. Although child marriages are still practiced in many parts of India, it is already prohibited as a taboo in the study areas.

Abandoned Taboos	Major Contributing Factor
Inter-caste/ Inter-Religious Marriage	Government Legislations, Urban Migration
Family Planning	Urban migration, Education, Mass Media, Government Legislations
Widow Remarriage	Education, Socio-Politico Pressure groups, Government legislations
Puberty-Related	Education, Mass Media
Menstruation-Related	Education

In the same way, polygamy that is widely practiced among the rich and affluent has become a social taboo due to education. Urban migration and education together with economic wellbeing have resulted in a taboo because of which having many children is prohibited in the study areas of Tamil Nadu. Mass media has influenced the rural population in such a high tone, partial nakedness which was an accepted customary practice vanish as social taboo emerges for semi-nakedness. Nudity in art, although not very prevalent in all the rural areas, still emerges as a taboo due to politico-religious pressure groups.

Conclusion: The study identifies that the emerging worldview regarding sex in rural communities is sensual that have been inculcated down through the centuries by the fusion of history from three ideological bases, religion and politics namely: i) sex is sacred, ii) sex is secret, and iii) sex is sin and shame. As the sex concept and worldview move from sacred to sensual, the gap between sexual norms and sexual behaviour widens. The study also identifies five sociological determinants and contributing factors that given birth to the contemporary sex norms and taboos namely: a) education, b) mass media, c) urban-migration, d) government legislations and e) pressure groups. There are socio-politico pressure groups as well as politico-religious pressure groups. One work for the abolishment of traditional meaningless taboo whereas the other reinforce new taboos taking back the society to conservative living. All these factors, in consequence, push the current rural community to abandon some sex taboos as well as adopt new ones.

Chapter **Three**

Culture & Human Behaviour[31]

Anthropology, psychology, and sociology are interrelated sciences that offer distinctive perspectives on the behaviour of individuals and groups. These sciences focus on the culture of the people and its influence on the individual as well as group behaviour and identity. The study of culture is an indisputable aid to understanding human behaviour as individuals as well as members of an ethnic community. From birth until death, our identity, personality and other human values are shaped by our culture.

Anthropologists together with psychologists and sociologists, in the last century, took attempts to apply Darwin's theory of evolution to every aspect of the human study. This gave rise to the Western thinking that the differences between human cultures are a series of stages as part of human evolution. This led further to the mythological concept 'civilized and primitive cultures'. Accordingly, the Western cultures were labelled as the most 'civilized' and Native American, African, Asian and Native Australian communities were labelled 'primitive and uncultured' (Murphy, 2007). Franz Boas was one of the leading figures to change this racist concept (Goodenough, 1996). In the psychological realm, culture and personality were studied by

[31]Portion of this chapter is taken from **Abyssinia in the New Millennium** (2015) ISBN: 978-1522757719 co-authored by **Mini TC** & **Alemayehu**.

Sigmund Freud, in his book *Totem and Taboo*[32]. He applied his psychoanalysis to the fields of archaeology, anthropology, and the study of religion. This helped him to understand his patients in their historical and cultural contexts. In the latter years, this study on culture and personality was popularized by Cora DuBois, Ruth Benedict and Margaret Mead and many other anthropologists.

Culture refers to common experiences which we share with the group or clan we live, that shape the way we view the world, interact and understand the world. Culture is expressed through various ways, mainly through language, customs, history, religion, taboo and totem, symbols, arts and architecture, gender roles, relationships, literature, fine arts, food and clothing, sport and entertainment, social and family structures, rituals and celebrations, myths and superstitions etc. Inculturation is the process of cultural transmission to infants and other new members.

Cora DuBois[33] in the 1930s, hypothesized that the adult personality is shaped by parenting and early childhood; how and when children are fed and weaned, the amount of love and affection they received. She conducted her research on Alor Island in Indonesia and found out that mothers resume gardening soon after the birth of their children, leaving their children with older women. In the custody and day-care of older women (grandmother or an elderly aunt) the children received little affection or attention and they were often brutally punished or teased (DuBois, 1960). This childhood experience leads to adult personalities who are hostile, suspicious, jealous and violent.

---

[32]Freud attempts to extend his analysis of the individual psyche to society and culture, in his book *Totem and Taboo* (1912-13). The psychology of primitive races bears marked resemblances to the psychology of neurotics; taboo customs parallel closely the symptoms of compulsion neurosis. Both totemism and taboo have their roots in the Oedipus complex, which lies at the basis of all neurosis, and also the origin of religion, ethics, society, and art.

[33]Cora Alice Du Bois (1903-1991) was an American cultural anthropologist who did some anthropological research among indigenous people in Indonesia from 1937 to 1939 and published her book *The People of Alor: A Social-Psychological Study of an East Indian Island* (1944), in which she argues strongly that culture plays a vital role in the development of personality.

Another leading figure in the field of culture and personality is Margaret Mead[34]. Her best-known study was on gender issues. In her book *Sex and Temperament in Three Primitive Societies* (1935), she proves that gender characteristics were not shaped by biology or genetic factors rather culture. Mead's research answers a basic question in cultural anthropology, *'why are we the way we are?* By explaining the association between childrearing custom and human development, she concludes that human behaviour is a by-product of culture. The cultural traits are learned and reinforced at different stages of life and development. Also, most of her conclusions are criticized, especially her studies on Samoan culture was strongly opposed by New Zealand anthropologist Derek Freeman[35].

Cultural psychologists have noted that some aspects of personality differ across cultural groups. For example, Americans and Asians have slightly different conceptions of self. American culture promotes a view of the self as independent. Americans tend to describe themselves in terms of personal attributes, values, and achievements, and they learn to be self-reliant, to compete with others, and to value their uniqueness. Many Asian cultures, such as those of Japan, China, and India promote a view of the self as interdependent. People from India tend to identify self-esteem as pride and often identify themselves in terms of which group they belong to. They learn to rely on others, to be modest about achievements. Similar differences can be seen in Africa also. The cultural psychology believes that culture

---

[34]Margaret Mead (1901-1978) was an American Cultural anthropologist and writer. In her *Coming of Age in Samoa* (1928) she argues for cultural determinism based on her life experience among the people of Samoa, a few tiny volcanic, tropical islands in the centre of the Pacific Ocean. She studied the indigenous culture that was still relatively undisrupted by the technologically developed world.

[35]John Derek Freeman (1916-2001) was a New Zealand anthropologist who was known for his strong criticism of Margaret Mead's work on Samoan people. He claims that Mead's findings are the result of a deception. Freeman found that it is common custom for Samoan's to exaggerate and joke when asked about sexual behaviour. Mead took the jokes as facts.

influences aggressiveness in males. However, research shows that in places where there are plentiful resources and no serious threats to survival, such as Tahiti or Sudest Island near New Guinea, males are not socialized to be aggressive (Murphy, 2007).

Culture also influences altruism. Research shows that children tend to offer support or unselfish suggestions more frequently in cultures where they are expected to help with chores such as food preparation and caring for younger siblings. Ideally, cultural psychologists acknowledge that not all members of a culture behave similarly. Variation exists within every culture, in terms of both individuals and subcultures. In this regard, we can make a difference between culture-specific psychology and cross-cultural psychology. Cross-cultural psychology highlights the similarity across different cultures whereas culture-specific psychology highlights the differences and uniqueness among cultures.

As modern cultures and technologies spread around the world, the traditional cultural practices, values diminish continually as younger generations slowly set aside their traditional culture, thinking and living and adapt to new lifestyles. However, the psyche still holds on the remnants of the past and, traditions. Sometimes it can create or lead to inner conflicts too. Therefore, scholars place greater emphasis on identifying indigenous cultures and knowledge. Organizations are being formed to preserve and foster traditional cultures, language, and knowledge of various groups of peoples.

Fast Food Indian Psyche: Indian culture is slowly changing due to various factors. Technology and globalization play a big role in the changing culture of India. Added to that, socio-political pressure groups that are becoming strong due to political support too, influence the Indian psyche.

In the grassroots, Indian psyche desires for instant coffee or fast food style decision making; always looks for quick fixes for any given problem rather than long term solid solutions. This is reflected in a variety of cultural praxis, behaviour, and lifestyles, not seeking permanent, concrete solutions rather short-sighted and looks for instant emotional solutions. Let me illustrate this with few examples.

Example: A girl was raped in a car in Delhi

Ideal solution: Women has the right to freedom, independence, and respect; educate men to respect women. Have stringent rules to punish the perverts and deviants quickly.

Indian quick-fix: Since the lady is raped in the car which had dark sunscreen in the windows, Indian Supreme Court orders to remove sunscreen stickers in the cars all over India so that we can avoid similar incidents in the future.

Example: People are hit on the road by speeding cars

Ideal solution: Roads are meant for cars and vehicles because they have paid road tax to use it; educate people not to walk on the road obstructing the movement of cars, provide tunnel way or footbridges for people to cross the road.

Indian quick-fix: Put speed breakers on the roads so that people can walk comfortably on the roads and no one will be hit by speeding cars. An annoying situation in Tamil Nadu: in a stretch of 7 KMS, there are 21 speed-breaker humps (much more than what one could see in Bhandipur National Park where animals move freely on the road).

Example: Boys make lurid comments on girl students in a college

Ideal solution: Educate boys to respect girls and behave properly.

Indian quick-fix: Students are not allowed to stand in the corridors during intervals and lunch break; if someone is found loitering in the corridors the teachers are accountable.

Example: There is a possibility of ragging by senior students

Ideal solution: Educate senior students to respect junior students and behave properly.

Indian quick-fix: Teachers are appointed all over the college, in the toilets, bike stand, coffee shop and on the road to supervise students, before the start of classes, during intervals, during lunch and after the end of classes.

Quick-fixes are not a real solution to any emerging or existing problem. Prevention and intervention strategies should be holistic. An ecological prevention strategy is highly recommended in which (a) an assessment of the individual, the environment, and the individual's adaptation to the environment, (b) the potential for change in the individual and the environmental systems and structures that surround the individual, should be considered. Using an eco-developmental framework will help to examine various external risk factors so that specific intervention strategies could be properly employed. What do we gain by quick-fixes?

Chapter Four

Musings on Indian Culture[36]

Indian culture looks at life as a whole. Culture is a nation's vital force contributing to its ideal fullness. Indian culture has both unity and diversity because it is a composite culture evolved through the centuries by the joint efforts of all people living in this vast subcontinent. People have humanity, tolerance, unity, secularism, strong social bond and other good qualities. We have a culture of people of all the castes and creeds living together conjointly. People in India are modern and follow all the changes according to the modern era. However, they are still in touch with their traditional and cultural values.

India has a rich culture and heritage. Culturally India has always been united in the sense that its people belonging to different races, speaking diverse languages, professing different faiths and following a variety of social ways have consistently acknowledged the primacy of spiritual and ethical values in human behaviour. Three significant values of our culture are tolerance, peaceful coexistence, and respect for pluralism.

---

[36]Contributed by **P. Willington Jebaraj** Ph.D, Corporate Lawyer, HR Specialist and CEO, Horeb HR Spectrum. He is a social activist, who has dedicated his life for imparting values. Dr. Willington moderated a Panel Discussion on Culture, Art & Gender at Sree Saraswathi Thyagaraja College, Pollachi on September 9, 2016.

Cultures have arisen and fallen in the international arena. Rome, Babylon, Greece, and hundreds of other cultures of the world are no more seen after their fall. But it is certainly a thing of exceptional pride for us that our Indian culture still remains intact.

Adoption: Although we must preserve our traditional culture and embrace it with all our passion, yet we must have some consideration for enriching and exchanging cultural values by being in touch with the rest of the world. Contact with the outside world has become inevitable for enrichment and advancement of our life. Late Pandit Nehru expressed that it was also India's way in the past to welcome and absorb other cultures of the world, and that is much more necessary when the entire world is becoming one united federation of entire humanity.

Emerging Trend: In recent times India's cultural identity is threatened by social conflicts affecting our peace, harmony, and growth. Factors, inter alia, contributing to this trend are:

- Increasing number of broken families, uncompromising disputes/differences/disharmony among family members
- Alcoholism and influence of movies and soap operas leading to alarming rise in perverted acts and behaviour
- Fall of moral values and moral disintegration
- Excessive socialization among younger generation
- Indifferent attitude
- Lack of empowerment and self-discipline
- Materialistic desires
- Diminishing human values
- Addiction to use of electronic gadgets in excess of genuine requirement
- Violence against women
- Evil social tendencies

The President of India has once said that 'evil social tendencies' could harm India's culture and that the values of love, harmony, peace, and sacrifice signify strengths of India's culture (PTI, February 24, 2013). It is very true that our rich culture should not be allowed to be decayed by evil social tendencies and other factors as seen above.

Intervention and Action: In order to preserve and enrich our cultural values , it needs intervention and action at multiple levels. The focus of the *society* should be on finding out root causes of the trend narrated above and then human values have to be injected into life steam since childhood as King Solomon wisely says, 'Train up a child in the way he should go, and when s/he is old s/he will not depart from it'.

A radical change in the *mindset of people* is necessary to give women their rightful place in society without any gender discrimination. People must be sensitized to treat women in a manner befitting the role played by them as loving and caring mothers, affectionate sisters, cute daughters and good companions.

The Role of Institutions: Institutions such as colleges, schools and welfare organizations should conduct series of seminars, workshops meetings at different places on various aspects of cultural values. They should discuss in depth the gravity, enormity, and dangers of dilution in the cultural value system and take steps to uphold values.

The Role of Media: The Madras High Court recently observed, "instead of inculcating good thoughts and moral values, filmmakers corrupt young minds by using vulgar lyrics in songs and projecting violence in movies. This affects our culture and morality" (The Hindu, September 4, 2016)· It is a serious and timely observation. Media including film industry can commit wholly to inculcate good cultural values. The Court also observed that the media is a powerful teacher whose teachings are never forgotten by people and therefore filmmakers should realize their responsibility for inculcating good thoughts in the minds of youth.

Home, sweet home is the first and foremost institution, where children learn the first lesson of humanity and social relationships. The family is the best place to inculcate positive values – like honesty, simplicity, modesty, sense of responsibility and respect for elders – amongst children and youth of both the sexes. Childhood is the most formative, educative and sensitive time in human life and most appropriate time for the inculcation of values because it can remain permanently and firmly in the delicate psyche throughout the life. Parents have to spend sufficient time with children in this formative stage not only for completing school homework but for orienting their own children into a meaningful life.

Last but not the least - the *individuals* have self-responsibility in preserving the culture. "The fault, dear Brutus, is not in our stars, but in ourselves," says William Shakespeare in Julius Caesar. Anne Frank says that parents can only give good advice or put them on the right paths, but the final forming of a person's character lies in their own hands, thereby emphasizing the role and responsibility of individuals in every walk of life.

Conclusion: Culture is not about *what* we do and surely not about whom we *follow*. It's about *why* we do something, and *how* we do anything. True to this saying, our Indian culture has stood the test of time and should continue to be so. Let not our behaviour permit anything to butt in into human value system. Let us commit ourselves to find meaning in the statement of Sri Aurobindo[37], "the ancient Indian race grew to astounding heights of culture and civilization, lived with a noble, well-founded, ample and vigorous order and freedom, developed a great literature, sciences, arts, crafts, industries, rose to high ideals of knowledge and culture, arduous greatness and heroism... discovered the profound truths of self and the world".

---

[37] Sri Aurobindo (1872–1950), is a noted Indian spiritual guru, was born in Calcutta, on August 15, 1872. He had his education in England. His knowledge of Western philosophy led him to understand and interpret Indian philosophy to the modern mind. After his studies at Cambridge, he started his life in India as a freedom fighter and was imprisoned for sedition. Later he took shelter in Pondicherry, a French territory, where he dedicated the rest of his life to spiritual pursuit. Aurobindo's philosophy is understood today as Integral Yoga Psychology (IYP) which promotes the highest levels of spiritual development, and of transforming human egoic consciousness into an organized centre for manifesting the Divine on earth. His concepts were criticised by some Western thinkers that he never fully assimilated the intersubjective (cultural) and interobjective (social) differentiations of modernity.

Chapter Five

Gearing for a Balanced Rearing[38]

- Who can smartly drive a high-CC sports bike?

- Who can hide the emotions and continue to be a strong person at any circumstance?

- Who can go for a film at night and return back home all alone?

The one possible answer from more than 90% of our population can be, "a boy".

From time immemorial, we have been spoon-fed with this gender bias between a boy and a girl child, in their function and behaviour at home, workplace, and society. We live in a generation where everyone is excited about updating technological gadgets, starting from latest Smartphone to brand new cars; added to that look for more comforts, like getting a Villa at the heart of the city. But, we miserably fail in updating ourselves in assigning genders roles and specific actions to be performed by each gender in the society. Generally, people have the mindset to appreciate a girl when she performs dance, when she is good at the kitchen, when she takes a caring role and above all when she stands out to be a huge pillar of emotional support. On the other hand, we feel great to see a boy as an adventure seeker, bike racer, breadwinner for a family and an ultimate decision maker. In no way, we are ready to admit the fact that this gender bias and gender stereotypes could actually be changed. There is only one qualification that we need to perform all these tasks: to be a human being.

[38]Contributed by **Ashwanth Kanna**, HOD, Psychology Department, Sree Saraswathi Thyagaraja College, Pollachi. The department organized an Academic Convention on Cyberpsychology on August 23, 2016 and a Symposium on Art, Culture & Gender on September 9, 2016 which paved the way for publication of this book.

Traditional, Cultural Outlook: Our cultural framework always needs a man to face problems and challenges in life and a female to give support, love, and care; not vice versa. Due to this societal expectation and male chauvinism, many females stick to the traditional roles; marginalised and even abused. This makes them lead a life, more for other members of the family and society, than for their own growth, development, freedom, and satisfaction. This difference in gender starts from birth, propagated by religion, nurtured by family and controlled at schools and colleges and the workplaces. There were no much problems in the past when women are not educated. Today this kind of dominance is seen in males, as husbands in the marital relationships, women tend to have a conflict with their spouses ultimately affecting the normal growth of children in the house. It makes the male child imitate and act like the father and throw upon aggressive tendencies towards the opposite gender. Poor parenting and domestic violence provide a fertile platform for antisocial tendencies to develop in male children. In the case of a female child, she just tends to suffer the same way she saw her mother suffer at home. This male dominance is reflected in schools and colleges as well as workplaces too and women are marginalised and harassed as the weaker sex.

Gender Bias & Discrimination: Another alarming gender issue committed against females is one sided love affair of men and the related violence. Men tend to show their failure in the form of aggression on females. At many workplaces, women are not given a permanent job because of certain factors like their wedding, maternity, etc. are considered a hindrance to work. The same does not hold good for a male. He can continuously serve at a workplace for a longer period.

Harikrishnan Nair write in Indian Express, *Gender bias is outdated, but then who cares* (July 11, 2015) identifies that despite people speak outwardly that gender bias no longer constitutes place in our society, it still prevails. He cites a research published in a Proceedings of National Academy of Sciences, which claims that science faculty of reputed universities had a bias for male candidates although both the gender possess similar qualifications. It has also been told that because of our stereotypical mindset, women are fixed with certain tasks and duties which are labelled as women job and only she can perform. This has been taken high by the virtual world starting from any book to movies where female are seen with same traditionally conceived conventional roles every sphere of the day and living.

In the olden days, it has been decided by a male and female to take up the tasks for their basic survival. Due to the muscular ability, men were involved in hunting the animals for food whereas women stayed back home and looked after the family. But today we no longer live in a world where men go for hunting for survival. The times have changed and the role of women today has been a lot more different. Yet women are identified with their soft-spoken traits as natural ability and are offered jobs of a teacher, nurse, doctor or an artist. But still, they are not preferred for certain jobs like a pilot, a driver or a scientist. In our traditional Indian families, for a girl child, importance is given to marriage rather than a profession. Even the parents are not ready to take a risk in adjusting their girl child for a better job and profession.

In another article cited at The Hindu titled, *"Bringing up boys"* (August 20, 2014), the author discusses the different ways in which boy children are raised at homes. The narratives given by parents were region specific as the article was based upon people at Kochi. The author advocates the hourly need to educate the boy child regarding girls and their approach towards them. Also, the article highlights the need for being sensitive to the issue of abuse in both genders.

From the perspective of a Psychiatrist John, we have over-involved parents who are good in advising the children but not to listen to them. He also commented the biased nature of parenting whereby girl children are asked to avoid the threatening situations and not to face it and this follows the upbringing pattern of being submissive and never reactive. But in the case of boys, the scenario sees a contrasting change and thus they are made to be bold and face all the problems with their parents giving them all the needed support and backing them up.

From a female perspective, even today girls tend to face problems of not being able to live a life by their own choice. If a girl turns out to be an adventure seeker and willing to undergo the adventurous tasks, she cannot do it just like that in the first place. It is mainly because of the restrictions she has to face from the family, relatives, friends and the society. This is the major hindrance to their freedom in an independent nation. The same freedom woes continue when a female wishes to pursue her higher studies, look for a thrilling job and settle for a marriage. Instead, they are made to undergo marriage first followed by either higher studies or job that too mostly depending upon the wishes of the in-laws. Thus, here the ultimate decision making for the girl rests not even in the hands of the parents now, but to their in-laws. Also, when there is a problem in females upon the conception of a foetus, the blame immediately rests on a female first blindly than on the males.

This whole scenario of gender discrimination can be changed at least by this generation of people. Whatever happened so far cannot be changed just like the saying, "there is no point in crying over the spilt milk". From now on, the good old pattern of keeping the boys and girls segregated based upon their socio-cultural norms and conditions could be revised. Both the genders deserve to be trained and excelled in all major art forms. There can be absolutely no harm in teaching martial arts to a girl or the classical dance to a boy. This very fact must be cultivated in the minds of "To Be Parent" Couples so that rejecting the desires and aspirations of today's young minds based on the gender could be reduced.

Treat the child right and show the path for their future so bright

Chapter Six

Architectural Psychology[39]

Psychology is directly related to culture, art, and architecture. Appropriate use of various artistic components such as colour, space and size have the capacity of enlightening the atmosphere. For example, a room with white coloured walls make us feel light and make the space brighter and more pleasurable to be inside. Architectural Psychology can be described as a branch of environmental or ecological psychology. It is the interaction between human and their environment. This includes spatial perception, orientation behaviour, living requirement and satisfaction. The architecture provides a sense of space and support to all type of human activities if used appropriately and it provides firmness, service, and delight. Architectural psychology is an important multidisciplinary field, bridging traditional psychology, engineering, architecture, domestic planning, and much more to assist people to design buildings and living spaces for better occupation. By understanding more about how people experience the built form, one can further take a more occupant-centred approach towards designing and engineering, which will lead to more truly innovative architectural designs.

---

[39]Co-authored by **Amrutha, M.S.**, Student of Architecture, Acharya Institute of Technology, Bangalore, who participated in a Panel Discussion on Culture, Art and Gender: the Indian Psyche, organised by the Department of Psychology, Sree Saraswathi Thyagaraja College, Pollachi on September 9, 2016.

Architecture is a form of human expression, portraying the psyche of the collective or individual designer. The father of analytical psychology Carl Jung[40] describes a building architecture as a structural diagram of the human psyche that conceives and creates. It is an established fact that art and architecture offers a vehicle for conveying our deepest unconscious thoughts of human beings.

A few decades ago, architects and construction companies were keen to engage psychologists for consultation in their designing process. Notable among them is David Canter, the author of many books on architecture, environment, and people, began his career as an architectural psychologist studying the interactions between people and buildings, publishing and providing consultancy on the designs of offices, schools, prisons, housing and other building forms. In his landmark publication, *Psychology for Architects* (1974) David Canter[41] explains the field of environmental psychology, analysing, explaining and understanding how people interact with the buildings and spaces around them. However, designers lost interest in applying psychology in engineering across the world and today it is difficult to find psychologists working together with architects. Designers very rarely engage themselves into the end user psyche. Of course, designers consider various human aspects in the designing process; however, building designs seldom use the knowledge of psychology directly. If

---

[40]Carl Gustav Jung (1875-1961) was a Swiss psychotherapist and one of the early followers of Sigmund Freud. In the latter period, Jung developed major theoretical divergence and their personal and professional relationship was broken. Jung's work has been influential not only in the field of psychology but also in philosophy, anthropology, archaeology, literature, and religious studies. He talks about two kinds of unconscious in a human being: personal and collective. The collective unconscious carries a lot of ancestral memories, probably many common elements we see in all humans. He also talks about archetypes which are images and thoughts which have universal meanings across cultures which may show up in dreams, literature, art or religion. Jung believes symbols from different cultures are often very similar because they have emerged from archetypes shared by the whole human race.

[41]David Victor Canter (born 1944) is a British psychologist who began his career as an architectural psychologist studying the interactions between people and buildings. Later he ventured into investigative psychology.

people don't like a particular environment they will not reside in it voluntarily and happily – be it a public space, a shopping centre or our home. But deciding what environment is pleasing and soothing or preferable is a difficult task. It is where the role of psychology and psychologists are needed.

There are ample researches to substantiate the role of psychology in the environment and engineering psychology. Christian Jarrett quotes a study conducted in 2011, for example, which was focused on curved versus rectilinear furniture. People were asked to view furniture in rooms and furniture with straight edges were rated as less appealing and approachable compared to curved ones. In another study, the psychologists at the University of British Columbia recruited six hundred subjects and had them carry out a variety of fundamental cognitive tests displayed against red, blue or neutral coloured backgrounds. The results were astonishing. People in the red background were much better at accuracy and attention as well as in spelling mistakes. This is attributed to the association of red with danger, which makes the people more alert and aware. Blue colour gave completely different results. People in the blue group performed worse on short-term memory tasks, but better in imagination. Psychologists at the Carlson School of Management found out the relationship between ceiling height and thinking style. When people are in a low-ceilinged room, they are much quicker at solving anagrams involving confinement; in contrast, people in high-ceilinged rooms excel at puzzles.

More findings from psychologist into engineering and architectural space, design and planning, explain further the inner psyche of people which is essential for healthy living space.

1)   When People with Alzheimer's having a private room with an own personal object around them will exhibit less aggression, anxiety and fewer psychotic symptoms.

2)   The Brain Development of premature babies can be disrupted by artificial lightning.

3)   People can be encouraged to drive through neighbourhoods more carefully using psychological

measures for example by making the roads narrow. Accordingly, by removing the street props and signs, altogether the speed of the vehicle can be reduced. The reason behind is that the without directions and boards may appear riskier for the drivers and finally he slowdowns his vehicle.

Similarly, the understanding of human psyche is essential in establishing uniqueness in workplace design, learning environments, healthcare facilities, residential environments and retail environments; each having its own specialities reflecting human mind, need and use.

Spatial cognition concerns the study of knowledge and beliefs about spatial properties of objects and events in the world. Cognition is about knowledge. In human, cognitive structure and process are part of the mind, which emerges from a brain and nervous system inside the body that exists in a social and physical world. Spatial properties include location, size, distance, direction, separation and connection, shape, pattern, and movement. Some major mechanism of structural design which affects human psyche are: building form, positive and negative space, colour, opening, open space, lighting, acoustics, sound construction, green technique, and landscape. People spend their better part of their day in a built environment and therefore much of their thought about space is directly intertwined with the architectural and urban form of their surroundings. Therefore spatial knowledge of our environment is an essential component of wellbeing, stress-free living and working.

When psychologists and engineers come together, they can make every environment a happy, stress-free, healthy and happy atmosphere.

Chapter Seven

Cyber Addiction: Mores to Medicine[42]

The word addiction comes from Latin *addico*, which means *to devote*. An addict is someone who is (excessively) devoted to something. Addiction involves a craving for something intensely, loss of control over its use, and continuing involvement with it despite adverse consequences. Addiction changes the brain, first by subverting the way it registers pleasure and then by corrupting other normal drives such as learning and motivation. Over time, the brain adapts the pleasure stimulant and more stimulation is needed to achieve pleasure and therefore a compulsive action is developed.

Internet, laptops, computers, iPads, tablets and Smartphone are wonderful inventions of this century. Connect the device to the internet and enter into the cyberworld, practically one can do anything. One can log on to play favourite games, watch movies, do shopping, banking, study, read and anything and everything. With the world wide open in front, it's easy to get caught up in it all. Similar to getting hooked on drugs, tobacco, coffee, or food many kids and teenagers are addicted to the Internet and it is difficult to stop doing even when there are exams or assignments to do. This is what psychologists call Internet Addiction Disorder (IAD). Educationalists and other social scientists are worried about this alarming situation.

---

[42]This paper was originally presented by Janetius at the Academic Convention-Addiction, Brain and Cyberpsychology (i-ABC) organized by the Department of Psychology, Sree Saraswathi Thyagaraja College, Pollachi on August 23, 2016.

When scientists started to study addictive behaviour in humans, the word addiction was already used in a very negative connotation. Even today an addict is looked down by the society. It is because, addiction is often identified with drugs and alcohol and therefore people who are addicted are viewed as persons with low moral acumen, lacking in willpower and decision making. From 1930's, the time studies on drug addiction and brain functioning slowly started to expand, addiction was never seen as a health problem. In the course of years, innovative and revolutionary discoveries about the brain functioning transformed the understanding of neurotic, obsessive and compulsive drug use, enabling psychologists, mental health, and other health professionals to respond differently to the problem. As a result, addiction is understood as a disease that affects both the brain and behaviour. The views that shaped the society's responses to drug abuse, treating it as a moral failing rather than a health problem is prevalent even today in which a strong emphasis is laid on punishment rather than prevention and treatment.

The brain is one of the most significant organs in the human body which manages our movements, actions, senses, thoughts, emotions, speech and all major activities. It is the connections inside the brain guide all organs to do what they are supposed to do. Neuroimaging or brain imaging is comparatively a new discipline within medicine, neuroscience, and psychology that employs a variety of procedures to directly or indirectly picture the construction, function and chemical actions and reactions of the brain and nervous system. Functional magnetic resonance imaging (fMRI), is the popular brain scan to show which parts of the brain are active to understand the relationship between activity in certain brain areas and specific mental functions.

Brain and Dopamine: Neurotransmitters in neurons are chemical messengers Neurotransmitters pass a message from one neuron to another. One specific neurotransmitter that plays a role in when pleasure is transmitted is *dopamine*. Despite the advances in neuroscience and related fields, many people do not understand fully how compulsive behaviour develop and why people become addicted to various lifestyles even if they know that it is harmful. Since addiction is primarily viewed as a disease today by mental health professionals, effective prevention and treatment approaches are identified to reduce such problems.

Today, the word addiction is not only restricted to drug, alcohol or tobacco use, it is also extended to any compulsive act like sex, the internet or any other problem behaviour as well. In this way, one can comfortably say that a student who skips a class because he is addicted to visiting places of worship and a student who is addicted to watching a movie on the opening day, a TV serial in the evening are equally mentally sick people. Of course, cultural practices and personal convictions also play a role in defining normal and sick behaviour.

The problem is that the addiction, in fact, changes the regular brain networks or neurotransmission pathways by which signals travel through the brain. Scientists explore and conclude that Internet addiction generally leads non-productive spending of precious, useful time for a variety of non-productive activities online. This leads to changes in the internal connections or networks inside the brain.

Addiction and Social Media: Scientists think dopamine, the pleasure chemical in the brain actually creates a want. Scientists think Dopamine causes us to seek, desire, and search. dopamine, the pleasure chemical in the brain actually creates a *want* when people are addicted to the internet and other cyber usages. Also, the brain develops tolerance to the pleasure giving tasks in the course of time. Recent studies have identified that brain develops tolerance not only when alcohol or drugs are used, it also develops for gambling, shopping, sex, etc.

Psychologists have come up with a new term IAD - Internet Addiction Disorder and the proposed identifying factors for this condition are loss of control over Internet use, resulting in marked distress, preoccupation, mood changes, tolerance, withdrawal, and functional impairments of social, occupational, and academic performance. Another proposed criterion is spending more than six hours a day on non-academic, non-business internet use for more than three months.

Attraction towards social media happens due to a basic need in a human being for self-presentation and relationships. Human beings are social beings and want to be associated with others; this need attracts people towards social media. Self-positioning oneself the way one want to be seen is a basic human tendency. Humans devote about 30 - 40% of all speech to talking about themselves. But online gives a chance to do that 80%.

Selfie Culture: Another phenomenon often seen among youngsters is *selfie-taking* and posting. Historically, portraits have been used for status and controlling the way our image is perceived. Before the invention of photography, artists are invited by influential people to draw their portraits, the way they wanted to look. This simple traditional practice is implied in *selfie-taking* and posting. 'Looking-glass self' is a psychological concept that explains that never truly see ourselves and we need our reflection from others in order to understand. Therefore people post things on the internet and look for acceptance and liking from others. Nostalgia is another reason people connect to social networks. Nostalgia is universal across all cultures and it gives us a sense of social connectedness, feelings of being loved and protected. Human beings cherish old memories and internet gives a provision to do that.

Conclusion: A dark side of internet poses a threat to people, especially youngsters. Social comparison, loss of privacy, cyber bullying and crimes, poor time management and addiction are threatening evils of cyber usage among the younger generation. Social media and internet could be used for better relationships, and enriching knowledge and various other positive functions. Addiction is very dangerous for growth, development and productivity and therefore the prudent use of technology and the related gadgets are highly recommended. Above all, a person who is addicted is not a person with low morals, rather s/he is sick and needs assistance and therapy. It is not the punishment that can transform an addict rather treatment.

Chapter **Eight**

Cyber Culture: Crimes & Corrections[43]

The presence of modern gadgets even in the remote corner of the rural area is the proof of modernization in our everyday life. Our increasing dependence on technology is spiralling day by day, which ultimately lead to many risks. Blaise Pascal the inventor of the calculating machine would not have imagined of the tremendous progress his original invention made during a short span of time, engulfing all areas of human activity. The technology marvel computer and the internet have created a new type of social problem and added a new concept in the criminal arena i.e. cyber crime, involving huge economic and human resource loss to the tune of millions per year. Apart from this monetary wastage, the corporate, the government and individuals spend a lot of their energy on cyber security. The problem involving cyber issues touch different areas of personal as well as social life.

Cyberspace and Psychosocial Issues: Addiction is a silent killer of social well-being of individuals as well as family in various forms; it could be alcoholism, substance abuse or internet addiction. A number of researches have been done by social scientists all over the world and they have come out with clear conclusions that internet addiction can

---

[43]Contributed by **P. Govindarajan** (Former DIG of Prisons), PhD scholar, Bharathiar University, Coimbatore. Govindarajan moderated a Group Discussion in the Academic Convention-Addiction, Brain and Cyberpsychology (i-ABC) at Sree Saraswathi Thyagaraja College, Pollachi on August 23, 2016. He is an active social worker; during his service as the DIG of various prisons in Tamil Nadu, he initiated several wellbeing activities for the prison inmates.

cause physical damage to the vital parts of the brain which is linked with emotion, decision making, and self-control; these damages are similar to that of substance abuse and cause brain damage in the same way as in the case of drug addiction. Internet Addiction Disorder (IAD) is one such malady mostly affecting the children and the youth who are glued to gadgets and cyberspace. There is an urgent need for prevention and intervention strategies to safeguard the youth who are silent victims of this cyber addiction.

Cyber usage has caused gender-related crimes in the form of Internet harassment and online threats targeting woman. They are on the rise that leads to fatal consequences such as victims going to the extent of ending their life, fearing social degradation of oneself and their family. Pew research centre survey in America reveals that 40% of the internet users experienced harassment and that too, women between ages 18-20 are more affected. Scholars have even begun to see these phenomena as a profound civil rights issue for women.

G. Krishnakumar, an advisor at the Centre for Educational and Social Studies, Bangalore, points out how internet addiction has become a public health issue and suggests that 'the ministry of Health and Family Welfare should consider creating a Pan India initiative similar to the National Addiction Management Services (NAMS) created by Singapore government'.

A coordinated effort by the AYUSH Ministry, HRD Ministry, and Telecom Ministry is the need of the day to save the public from the evil effects of internet addiction. A Japanese innovative 'Internet Fasting Camp' which encourages real communication with other children and adults and motivate children to spend much less time online is noteworthy and could be initiated in India too. The meaning and the concept of crime corresponds with the evolution of society from primitive to modern times. This shows a marked change from agrarian to an industrial society with complex factors of crime, criminal and the victims, whose interest must be safeguarded by the collective action of society in the form of state interventions.

Sociologist Emile Durkheim[44] in his treatise *Crime is a normal phenomenon* says, "a society composed of persons with angelic qualities would not be free from violation of the norms of that society. In fact, crime is a constant phenomenon changing with the social transformation" (Hamlin, 2009). A change in the lifestyle brings forth a different set of norms and rules in the society, giving way to enactment of the new statute to safeguard the innocent from the social abrasions. Donald Taft says 'crime is a social injury and an expression of subjective opinion varying in time and place'.

The fruits of science have improved our standard of living, at the same time the evil mind find the seeds of poison within the sweet fruit. The recent news items in the mass media reveal a different face of the society, which is wrongly used as a double edged weapon. Criminologist broadly classified crime into blue collar crime and white collar crime. It is E. H. Sutherland[45] who spoke at length about the concept of white collar crime first time in 1941 and says "Besides the traditional crime such as assault, robbery, dacoity, murder, rape, kidnapping and acts involving violence, there are certain antisocial activities which the persons of upper strata carry on in course of their occupation or business" (Croall, 2001). Though cyber crimes are committed by educated persons, it won't fix in within the narrow limits demarcated by Sutherlands. The peculiar nature of cybercrime is such that they can be committed anonymously and far away from the victims without being present there. These include theft of communication services, industrial espionage, dissemination of

---

[44]David Émile Durkheim (1858-1917) was a French sociologist, social psychologist and philosopher often referred as the father of sociology. One of the main arguments for Durkheim's theory is that since crime is found in all societies, it must be performing necessary functions otherwise it would disappear in an advanced society. Therefore crime itself serves a social function.

[45]Edwin Hardin Sutherland (1883-1950) was an American criminologist. He is considered as one of the most influential criminologists of the 20th century. He is best known for his definition of white-collar crime and differential association, a general theory of crime and delinquency. Although Sutherland's theories received wide praise, his critics maintained that he failed to explain both the development of the first criminal and why some people with excessive exposure to criminal behavioural patterns do not commit criminal acts.

pornographic and sexy offensive material in cyberspace, electronic money laundering and tax evasion, electronic vandalism, terrorism and extortion, telemarketing frauds, illegal interception of telecommunication.

The first reported case in cybercrime dates back to 1820 when a group of labours destroyed an advanced automated loom, fearing that there will be retrenchment when the automated machines begin to function. In India telecom act 1996 is the first statute which regulates the use of telecom services before that Indian Penal Code 1868 has provisions for dealing with offences related to, or with the computer. Apart from IT Act 2000, there are special laws like copyright act and trademark act etc., are there to deal with cyber crime. Cyber Crimes in India are registered under two different acts, the IT Act and the Indian Penal Code (IPC). The cases registered under the IT Act include:

- Tampering computer source documents (Section 65 IT Act)
- Loss /damage to computer resource/utility (Section 66 (1) IT Act)
- Hacking (Section 66 (2) IT Act)
- Obscene publication/transmission in electronic form (Section 67 IT Act)
- Failure of compliance/orders of Certifying Authority (Section 68 IT Act)
- Failure to assist in decrypting the information intercepted by Govt Agency (Section 69 IT Act)
- Unauthorized access/attempt to access to protected computer system (Section 70 IT Act)
- Obtaining license or Digital Signature Certificate by misrepresentation / suppression of fact (Section 71 IT Act)
- Publishing false Digital Signature Certificate (Section 73 IT Act)
- Fraud Digital Signature Certificate (Section 74 IT Act)
- Breach of confidentiality/privacy (Section 72 IT Act)

On the other hand, cases are also registered under the IPC and those include:

- Offences by/against Public Servant (Section 167, 172, 173, 175 IPC)
- False electronic evidence (Section 193 IPC)
- Destruction of electronic evidence (Section 204, 477 IPC)
- Forgery (Section 463, 465, 466, 468, 469, 471, 474, 476, 477A IPC)
- Criminal Breach of Trust (Section 405, 406, 408, 409 IPC)
- Counterfeiting Property Mark (Section 482, 183, 483, 484, 485 IPC)
- Tampering (Section 489 IPC)
- Counterfeiting Currency / Stamps (Section 489A to 489E IPC)

Year All India record	IT Act		IPC	
	Cases Registered	Persons Arrested	Cases Registered	Persons Arrested
2011	1791	1184	422	446
2012	2876	1522	601	549
2013	4356	2098	1337	1203
Total	9023	4804	2360	2198

The numbers of cases registered under the IT Act and IPC have been growing continuously. The cases registered under the IT act grew at more than 50% in 2012 & 2013. The cases registered under the IPC in 2013 more than doubled from 2012. A similar trend is observed in the number of persons arrested. The government also accepts that with the introduction of technologies, devices including smartphone and complex applications, and rise in usage of cyberspace for businesses, cyber crimes are on the rise in the country.

The Growth of Cyber Crimes vs. Internet Subscribers: Though the growth in cyber crimes & Internet Subscriber base are not similar, they follow a similar trend. While cyber crimes have grown at more than 50% in both 2012 & 2013, the internet subscriber base has grown at 27% in 2012 and at 53% in 2013. It is evident that cyber crime is growing with increasing internet penetration whereby electronic communication has become easier. Since cybercrimes need technical expertise, the enforcing authorities have to train its staff in this ever widening cyber world. Though the number of trained staffs are limited, the number of cases registered and persons arrested increased over the period of past five years.

The "2016 Cost of Data Breach Study India" reported that the average total cost of a data breach paid by Indian companies increased by 9.5%, while the per capita cost increased by 8.7% and the average size of a breach grew by 8.1%. KPMG survey report 2014 has classified cyber attackers may be internal/external and suggested seven security measures save from cyber attacks, they are;

- Antivirus Software
- Antispam Filters
- Firewalls
- Intrusion detection system
- Encrypted files
- Encrypted login/session
- Biometrics, Smart cards/tokens

Cyber Crimes and Correctional System: Every correctional system of today has to deal with cybercrime and cybercriminals. It has to device an up to date correctional programs to treat the cybercrime offenders. The criminal justice administrative system of today selectively apply different types of treatment philosophy's, i.e. the deterrent theory of punishment or to use the alternative method of treatments like community service or day reporting centres which provides opportunities to individual to support his family financially at the same time pay back the society for the harm done by him without the evil effect of stigma arising out of incardination.

Cyber Security: To combat cyber attacks, India appointed its first chief information security officer (CISO) to tackle the situation more effectively. The creation of National Cyber Security Agency (NCSA) is on the progress. In the world arena, India and the U.S. agreed to cooperate on cyber security issues. In 2015, India, and U.K. agreed to establish a cyber security training centre of excellence and India made agreements with Malaysia and European Union in cyber security cooperation.

Conclusion: To treat the malady in the cyberspace system, a multi-dimensional approach has to be resorted, such as proactive, preventive and reactive curative methods and at the same time giving much importance to prevention which will result in avoiding loss and suffering. Through various awareness program among youth, especially among students, we can prevent cyber crimes a lot. Another area is the prevention of cyber addiction. Cyber addiction could lead to cyber crimes. Teaching students the correct use of electronic gadgets is yet another area parents and teachers can work together. If similar efforts are taken in creating awareness among the Indian young, the cyberculture can be channelized towards positive energy for a better 2020 digital India.

Chapter Nine

Fashion & Dressing Culture[46]

India today is becoming a fertile hub for budding fashion designers as youngsters are becoming increasingly fashion conscious, owing to exposure to media influence. The purpose of this study is to evaluate the dress colour and dressing style preference of rural adolescents. The study conducted among college students from rural areas of Perur, Pollachi and Udumalpet taluks of Coimbatore and Tiruppur districts suggests considerable gender differences in regard to fashion consciousness, preference of colour and choice of dress on different occasions.

How many distinct colours and shades can the human eye distinguish or the number of colours perceptible to the human eye? The International Commission on Illumination suggests that the human eye can detect approximately 2.38 million colours. The ability of the human eye to distinguish a meaningful difference in colour tone and shade is limited by the visual capability of the individual. The powerful influence of colour regulates our choices from selection of a phone we use, the bike we ride, the car we drive, the food we eat, clothes we wear and the house we dwell. Preference for particular

[46]Co-authored by **Shilpa, S.T**, Student, Department of Management Studies, NIT, Trichy. Originally this paper was presented in a National Conference in 2015.

colour or dress is a deeply rooted emotional response which may not offer any apparent rational answer. Psychologists down through the centuries maintain that colour preference is related to human personality and colours have an impact on our moods, feelings and behaviour. Colour or colour preference is a silent vibration giving specific meaning and message to the person who uses and, it sends a strong message to people who see (Mahnke, 1996). Scientific studies in the field of colour psychology have found that different colours can provoke very different reactions in people. Faber Birren (1997), a pioneer in the field of colour study, argues that colours affect our personality and mood and, it is possible to make precise judgments about the meaning of colour preferences and their revelations of personality traits.

Although individual differences are emphatically pronounced in perception and preference of colours, psychologists figure out some personality attributes behind this differences and also commonality among choices (Ritberger, 2005). There are days a person prefers warm shades and s/he prefers cold and pale shades on certain other occasions. Added to that, people prefer some colours appropriate to certain occasions even if they do not like the colours and shades altogether. While some people hate certain colours, there are people who prefer such colours in their day to day dressing. For example, people are biased and have stereotypic concepts about the use of black colour in the society, often it is associated with death, mourning and sadness. However, there are people who find it classy, fashionable, and professional and even attractive (Rebecca Willis, 2011). A study on Carl Jung's (1962) ancestral inheritance, collective unconscious and its role on social labelling of colours are far from the scope of this study, however, the unconscious motives behind colour preference is easy for comprehension. A good judgment of the way colour and personality interact can help us choosing appropriate clothing, and making our daily interactions pleasant and pleasing to others.

Human Eye and Colour Vision: Human vision is one of the most complex visual systems in the evolution of species giving humans the ability to see physical environment. Humans, apes and some monkey species have trichromatic vision, with eyes containing three colour receptors, sensitive to blue, green and yellow-red whereas many species of mammals only have blue and green receptors, and can distinguish fewer colours[47] (Kleiner, 2004). The receptor cells rods and cones in human eye which take light rays as physical stimuli inside and transforms them into electrical and chemical signals to the brain. There are roughly 120 million rods and 6 to 7 million cones in the human eye. Colour sensors cones respond to a broader colour of red, green, and blue (RGB). These three colours are called primary colours. All other colours in between are perceived as different linear combinations. The cones also have three sets which correspond to the red, blue and green light that fall on the retina and the perception of colours resulting from their combinations are called secondary colours.

Colour vision plays an important role in both perception and communication. Colour perception is a complex thing which depends not only on the wavelength of the light that the sensors in the eye receive, but also the circumstances or environment in which we perceive, such as background lighting, familiarity, and lighting in the surroundings. The chemicals in the objects reflect the pale sunlight in a particular wavelength and the rods and cones which are stimulated in a specific way send the message to the brain to identify in Red, Green, Blue (RGB) variations as colours. Colour blindness is a vision deficiency in which a person is not able to differentiate or distinguish colour shades. There are different causes of colour blindness, the majority of it is genetic and has been inherited from their mother. Colour blind people are generally able to see as clearly as normal people but unable to differentiate red, green or blue shades fully; they are also people who can't see any colour at all. Colour vision

---

[47]Humans see more colours than some animals. Dog and cat see fewer and weaker colours. However, some animals see colours which human eye can't see. For example, spiders and many insects can see ultraviolet that most humans cannot see; so also snakes are able to see infrared light. Bulls, along with all other cattle, are colour-blind to red. In bullfights, the bull is likely irritated not by the muleta's red colour, but by the movement as the matador whips it around.

deficiency affects roughly 1 in 12 men (8%) and 1 in 200 women globally (Robin, 2014).

Colour Psychology: The following table collected from various sources gives a general picture of some of the popular psychological interpretation for different colours.

White	Symbol of purity, balance, unity harmoniously Popular in wedding gowns & events symbolising peace In fashion and daily setting, it is jarring, unfriendly Culturally in India widows are given white colour dress; symbolising austerity and cultural religious connotations
Black	Absence of light and colour Western cultures it symbolises death; associated with mourning and grief, hatred Symbolises powerful and provocative in dressing Wearing black makes impression and projects seriousness
Orange	Odd colour, provokes mixed reactions; feelings of warmth and enthusiasm Variation brown creates comfort, relaxing & security Indian culture it is the colour of austerity used by monks Today associated with fundamental religious view in India
Purple	Feels soothing and peaceful and can help relieve anxiety Traditionally seen with royalty & nobility, an exotic colour Purple tie gives dash to your look; however, a purple suit probably looks weird
Green	Colour of life and nature, often associated with health and prosperity Promote relaxation, peace, and calm; stimulates a restful, secure and balanced feeling Green could make people think of you as positive and relaxed
Pink	Western culture made pink a feminine colour Symbolizes innocence of childhood, gentle side of human nature and youth Thinking life should be constantly romantic and generous
Yellow	Tends to promote optimism, energy, alertness Happiness and joy in people And associated with adventurousness People use this colour to promote optimism and enjoyment Wearing a yellow dress can brighten up the day
Blue	Represent sky, ocean; soothing to body & reduce heart rate Good colour to use in a bedroom to lull to sleep Associated with wisdom, loyalty and royalty
Red	Intense and arousing colour associated with love and hatred Denotes extroversion of a person with desire, appetite, will live life fully Aggressive, impulsive, quick to release feelings and emotions Red lipstick, dress, or tie can attract attention

Traditionally colours are identified from the rainbow and the seven colours of the spectrum. Today the three predominant colours identified for computer based display are RGB or Red, Green and Blue. By varying the amount of each of these colours, the human eye can be tricked to see a spectrum of colours, including white and black. Because these primary colours occur frequently in nature, they have corresponding psychological properties that can change our behaviour and emotions. Psychologists in the field of colour and personality or colour psychology bring out the following description of various colours.

Fashion and Dressing: Fashion is a general term for a popular style or practice, especially in clothing, hairstyle, footwear accessories, makeup, etc... Fashion refers to a distinctive and customary trend in the style with which a person dresses, as well as to prevailing styles in behaviour. Popularly it denotes costume and dressing style of people. Clothing serves as much more than covering and protection. It is a means of communication to reflect social status, lifestyle.

Down through the centuries, people tend to dress according to occasion and need. The clothing style can be divided into different categories: it could be traditional, casual, trendy, casual and professional or elegant. Some are designed for comfort; some clothes are for informal occasions and emphasize relaxation and often referred as casual wear. Some clothes bring seriousness, youthfulness, superiority, attitude, culture and status. Among students, it mostly suggests the sense of dress.

Adolescents allocate more time for their public appearance than to studies. The peer influence, hero-worship which become part of adolescent identity creation is the primary reason why adolescents aspire for more fashion concerns than any other age group. Colleges generally project the picture of the current trend in fashion. As soon as adolescents join college, a spectacular change occurs in their self-appearance consciousness. Therefore it is normal for a college student who is in the identity creation stage of Erikson's psychosocial development[48] to look for trendy dress choices (1968). When a particular style of dress comes in vogue or used by film stars and models, it is blindly followed by college students (Pathak, 2013). Fashion trend today does not give precedence to comforts and practicality. Sometimes the dress, that goes beyond modesty and simplicity, which does not allow someone to sit or walk properly, is attracted by youth. Untidy, shabby looking hairstyles, which are trendy, attract adolescents.

This paper is prepared by collecting data from 536 college students from Perur, Pollachi and Udumalpet taluks of Tamil Nadu using convenient sampling (those who were willing to participate). Simple statistical analysis, rank order and significant differences were identified.

Results and Discussion: This study on the psychology behind colour and fashion, among rural college students, was aimed at identifying the major colour preference and dressing style. A total of 536 students were studied (34% of the students studied were boys and 66% girls). For the purchase of a dress, 54% of the boys did everything by themselves. For example, they chose the colour and style of their dress. But 60% of the girls report that the choice was done by their parents. As per the choice of colour in their costumes, the highly favoured colours of the boys are black, orange and white shades whereas for girls it is pink, white and violet. One commonality seen among rural boys and girls is white. This shows the traditional, conservative

---

[48]Erik Homburger Erikson (1902-1994) was a German-born American developmental psychologist, known for his psychosocial development theory. His theory talks about eight stages – from birth to death. His ideas were greatly influenced by Freud and goes along with Freud's theory of personality (id, ego, superego). He emphasized the role of culture and society and the conflicts that can take place within the ego itself, whereas Freud emphasized the conflict between the id and the superego. Erikson extends Freudian thoughts by focusing on the adaptive and creative characteristic of the ego and expanding the notion of the stages of personality development to include the entire lifespan.

outlook among the rural population. The following table shows the preferred and less preferred dress colours.

	Male	Female
	Black	Pink
Favourite dress colours	Orange	White
	White	Violet
Less preferred dress colours	Red	Yellow
	Yellow	Black

Psychologists understand the preference for white colour in many people is a recall of their youth and innocence. Probably the preference for white colour tells the innocence of rural life and thinking. As for the dislike of other colours, there is gender difference which is also noticed. Boys although prefer red colour to impress people by their dress, generally dislike red and yellow shades in their common choice. Girls, on the other hand, dislike yellow and black. A commonality seen in both boys and girls is a dislike for yellow. Colour yellow is associated with happiness and joy. This is also identified with optimism, energy, alertness, and adventurousness. However, rural students do not like this colour.

Psychologists argue that the colours one dislike can tell a lot about personality, often reflecting weaknesses and vulnerabilities (Ritberger, 2005). The most disliked colour will relate to areas in life that need to be given attention or past hurts that need to be healed. Freudian psychologists associate unconscious and childhood memories for this dislike. Hatred for a colour or rejecting a colour altogether can create imbalances in life. They further suggest people, to incorporate a disliked colour into life, by using them in small amounts to balance one's energies.

White is the colour favoured by both the gender to impress people and to look nice. On many occasions like visiting a temple, participating in functions at home and out, girls prefer the traditional female colour pink together with white. Boys look for more aggressive black or red. This is a well-pronounced gender difference. The extraversion, desire, appetite and dynamism linked to red colour is the popular favourite of boys. This shows boys like to be somewhat aggressive, impulsive, athletic, and quick to release their feelings and emotions. On the contrary, girls look for pink and rose shades. In the Western culture, pink is often referred as a feminine colour, stressing vulnerability and child-like emotions. It also symbolizes the gentle side of human nature, health, abundance and youth. Psychologists suggest two types of people like pink a) people who led a very sheltered life and, b) those who seek to regain the innocence of childhood. Overall, in pink, there is affection, delicacy and an inner conviction, devoid of trials and tribulations.

Dress preference for Occasion	Boys	Girls
Dress to look nice & impress people	White	White
	Red	Pink
Going out with friends	White	White
	Black	Pink
Temple/religious functions	White	White
		Pink
Marriage/family functions	White	Pink
		Red
		Violet
Tour/outings	Black	Black
	Red	Pink

When asked about the dressing style, the rural college boys prefer modern trendy dress as the dominant style whereas girls want to be in casual and relaxed styles. Boys select casual and relaxed dressing style as their secondary choice whereas girls go for traditional and classical style. Modern and trendy styles denote the consciousness of the boys in the latest, cutting-edge fashion designs in clothing. Impressing the attention of others seen in adolescent identity creation, elaborated by Psychologist Erikson is clearly seen among boys in their trendy fashion and personality. Trendy also describes the boys who prefer the latest, most up-to-date fashion available, often used by film stars in popular movies. As regards the casual and relaxed dressing style of girls, it is evident that the girls look for comfort, practicality and ease which are important factors in their dress. It clearly reflects the rural mood that they do not venture into modern trends and cutting edge styles. Psychologists define people who prefer casual style as those who are reserved, unpretentious, approachable, easy-going and down-to-earth. Another choice of girl students - classic and traditional outfit preference- tells about people who wish to be simple, more conservative and the style pronounces the message 'neat and tidy person'. Both casual and traditional style suits well and projects clearly the personality of rural mindset.

Conclusion: The study suggests that there are considerable gender differences in fashion consciousness, colour preference and choice of dress on different occasions. College boys prefer white shades more than anything else whereas girls prefer white and pink coloured costumes. Boys tend to favour trendy and modern outfit whereas girls choose casual and relaxed costumes. Boys take the freedom to choose their dressing materials whereas a girl's choices are limited by the interference of parents. Further studies could be done in broader avenues like demographic variables, urban – rural differences and place of education for a detailed understanding of dress and fashion consciousness.

Chapter **Ten**

Commercials & Stereotypes[49]

India was initially a place associated with deep-rooted spirituality and rejection of materialism. However, the turn of the century marked a change in the values, beliefs and habits of the modern consumer. An estimated 200 million people who belong to the middle-class are the targets of all the multinationals now. It is because one fifth of the world under 20 populations is in India.

All marketing gurus agree that the Indian society is a complex audience to cater to, more so in the case of advertising. There are topics and themes which are not supposed to be mentioned or displayed, but at the same time, some clever advertisers have no qualms in using those taboo topics as a tactic to garner more attention. In an increasingly emerging consumerist society, celebrities and body images are used as a way to reach people. Although such images can be deceiving and not plausible for the masses, the concept of an ideal body or an ideal image still strikes a chord in the people. This is where this paper tries to focus on – how Body Image is kept as a focal point in many advertisements in India and how inadvertent they are

Gender Stereotypes: The popular belief today that women should have flat stomachs and curvy body and, men should be muscular. There are ideals common to both genders – being tall and fair skin, having white

[49]Co-authored by **Shilpa**, **S.T**, Business Analyst, a MBA graduate & Gold Medallist, National Institute of Technology, Trichy.

teeth etc. What used to be good-to-have has now become must-have for every teenager and young adult.

Stereotyping Men & Women: In today's world, there aren't many advertisements that don't include either an image of a young attractive woman or a woman that is busy doing housework while her husband is nowhere to be found. These types of images portray women only as sex objects or as subservient housewives to their husbands. Though on the rise, it is still very rare to see a woman portrayed in a position of power in advertisements.

Advertisers are still under the impression that "sex sells" and that women are still the only ones doing housework. The objectification of women has for the most part always existed in advertisement and has been the driving force behind many feminist movements. Though in recent years, women have started to use sex appeal as a way of empowerment and therefore don't get as offended by some of the advertisements of today; they still have strong feelings about the way women are objectified in the advertisements we see daily on TV and in magazines. The most classic example is a fairness cream, which tries to sell that only fair women are attractive. Many dusky women have been buying this product based on the misconception that skin colour defines beauty.

Another recent advertisement for a leading telecommunication company is a prime example. In the advertisement, a woman is shown resolutely giving a work deadline to a man in the opening scene. After showing a warm disapproval, the man silently moves out of the woman's cabin to finish the assigned job and works late into the night. On the other hand, his boss – the assertive woman, leaves for home. After reaching home, the woman then calls up her husband, who is nobody else but the same man from the office (her subordinate) and persuades him to come home, telling him about the delicious four-course meal she has cooked for him. The debate lies intact that if a woman is smart, successful and confident enough to lead her way, then why is it necessary for her to cook for her man at home after spending almost as much time in the office as her husband or other co-workers do?. Similarly, many advertisements show women as sensual objects devouring food items or drinking juice and seducing men. What tickles the mind is that often the sensual picture described and the product would have no connection to each other. It becomes quite clear that the female lead is cast only to add a clichéd wow factor. It doesn't penetrate the minds of consumer that the storyline is irrelevant or that the ideal image portrayed is far from reality.

With the advent of Photoshop, and with retouching now prevalent even when famous people featured in the advertisements do not want photo editing, the images of women that are flawless, and anatomically impossible, are harmful on so many levels because men are told to look for this sort of ideal women and young ladies are told to become like them.

Advertisers are not hesitant to portray men as objects either. We have tall, fair handsome men vying for the attention of women – not necessarily unmarried. Whether it be a fairness cream, soap or deodorant, men are equally subjected to a fake body image. A disproportionate number of buff, often-shirtless actors are lately popping up in advertisements for everything from salad dressing to air fresheners - in other words, consumer products not normally associated with sexual imagery. While some see it as a turning of tables on men and good-natured gender-reversal, it still bears scrutiny since it propagates a stereotype that men should be all that is shown.

What actually inspires incredulity is the advertising series by a famous deodorant and soap company which portrays that adultery is inevitable when using the product. These hyped advertisements persistently tell the masses that women and men are easy to get – all that is needed is a seductive body spray that makes them more attractive to the opposite sex.

- Is this the real portrayal of our modern society?

- Do women really appear from nowhere and get attached to men, based on what deodorant or toothpaste they use?

Both men and women who star in advertisements are subject to the 'Perfect Body' image. Even though the fact cannot be contested that the advertisements are not meant to teach morality to people, but then, this is also true that it has certain responsibilities towards the society because it reaches to millions of homes and influences people, directly or indirectly. Marketers need to understand that the incessant exposure to such messages does have an impact on the viewers and the society at large.

Chapter Eleven

Celebrities & Commercials

Advertisements are considered the nervous system of the business world. The human nervous system is created to give sensations from external objects, so also the advertisements are focused on awakening the people about various products that come to the market. The main objective of advertising is to attract the attention of potential buyers. In this modern consumerist society, advertisement therefore becomes essential to stand out in the competition of ever increasing consumer market. Companies are trying various ways and means of reach out to people to get the attention by various creative and innovative means. As IT field becomes the main road of communication today, viral marketing, cloud marketing, and various other marketing techniques are used to advertise the products and to stretch out to consumers. In view of gaining more attention and appeal from people, companies use celebrities as an effective method of marketing strategy (Tripp, Jensen & Carlson, 1994).

Advertisements are meant to attract the people towards their products. They are made in such a way that, they try to capture the minds of viewers. Marketers use mass media as an effective weapon for canvassing. The combined audio and visual features of television make it; stand out from the rest of mass Medias. The advertisers find television more effective rather than other medias to reach customers since it is more common in rural and urban households. It is presumed that social behaviour and purchasing behaviour are influenced by the advertising.

History of Advertisement: The ancient method of advertising used was the word of mouth which is even today a powerful advertising strategy all over the world. The first known advertisement printed appeared in March 1648, however, advertising in magazines began only in recent times. Although many psychologists worked in persuasive techniques in capturing the attention of people in selling products, the familiar advertising strategies used today, are the by-product of American Psychologist J. B. Watson[50] (Goodwin, 1999). The first psychologist to study scientifically the process of persuasion was Gale Harlow in 1895, who theorised that affective and cognitive aspects, issue involvement, personal influence and unconscious attitude formation were the processes of persuasion leading to buying (Faglio, 2012). In his writing 'the theory and practice of advertising', Scott (1903) identified people as highly suggestible and obedient and initiated a feedback system, asking the customers to complete coupons and mail it back to the company (Benjamin & Baker, 2004). Hollingworth was yet another pioneering psychologist who studied 'effective advertising'. He identifies capturing the attention as the key to advertising. He further elaborated that giving a message to make the customer remember it, leads to purchase power in effective advertising (Faglio, 2012). J. B. Watson was the man behind introducing various advertising techniques by the use of psychology. Watson was a behaviourist from Johns Hopkins University who took the world on his side by his classic experiment 'Little Albert'. His

---

[50]John Broadus Watson (1878-1958) was an American Behaviourist psychologist. His classical experiment "Little Albert" on conditioning gave him a place among prominent psychologists. His father was an alcoholic and abusive person left the family for another woman; his mother, a pious conservative Baptist lady was a victim of domestic violence. Watson as a teen had his own difficult times with law and order and was arrested several times for fighting. In spite of his predisposition for alcohol, excessive partying and aggression he was able to take up studies. In 1908, Watson became a faculty at Johns Hopkins University. However, he had to leave the teaching position due to his scandalous affair with a graduate student-assistant and co-researcher Rayner, whom he married after divorcing his first wife, following the scandal. This scandal and other allegations on sex-experiments, made it impossible for him to take up teaching career and eventually entered into advertising career.

entrance to the field of advertisement was a mere accident. The dismissal from Hopkins University following a scandal forced Watson to enter into the advertising business for survival. He took a job with the J. Walter Thompson advertising agency and in 1935 Watson switched jobs to become an advertising executive at the William Esty Company where he remained until his retirement in 1945. Though it was accidental, Watson used his theory of behaviourism and studied emotions of fear, rage, and love in his experiments to improve the effects of advertising.

Almost all the psychologists focus on persuasion as the key in advertising and the key to change the attitudes of people towards buying. Persuasion techniques have been studied by social psychologists early in the 20th-century. The ultimate goal of persuasion is to convince the consumers to internalize the persuasive argument and adopt this new attitude as a part of their core belief system. One common technique used for persuasion is the use of authority. This is based on the idea that people will respect the opinions of someone whom they admire or accept as a hero or a knowledgeable person. People feel better knowing that someone with authority has recommended what they are about to buy. Of course, the authority person has to have expert knowledge in that particular field. Would anyone buy certain toothpaste because a car salesman recommended it?

Indian Psyche and Celebrity Endorsements: India is a country of diversity in cultural practices, languages, and customs. Joint family, dependence on parents, arranged marriages, male dominance, devotion, religious affinity are strong cultural and traditional factors that dominate every sphere of living. Cult status is given to film stars, cricket players and popular personalities and hero worship is rampant. Television serials have become part of Indian household talks and cricket games are highly sought serious part of life than work and profession for many. This Indian worldview is reflected in the marketing and advertisement arena too where film stars and sportspersons (mainly cricket stars) are given high celebrity status and perceived as attractive, talented and extraordinary personalities (Taleja, 2008).

McCracken (1989) sees celebrity endorsement in marketing as "any individual who enjoys public recognition and who uses this recognition on behalf of a consumer good by appearing with it in an advertisement ... thus they bring their own culturally related meanings." The characteristics which differentiate celebrity from the common people are popularity, a high degree of recognition in a society or culture, an a attention grabber and high degree of fame in their respective field.

Celebrity endorsement is a multimillion rupee business in India[51]. People like to see celebrities and their heroes in commercials and some stars are seen selling more than one product. A celebrity may appear in commercials in many ways: as a spokesperson or a salesman, an endorser even though s/he may not be an expert in the brand, provides testimony about the personal experience of the product and its superiority, or an actor in the advertisement. This has been classified by McCracken (1989) as explicit mode in which the celebrity announces the endorsement of a product; implicit mode in which the celebrity uses verbal or physical communication for the product and, imperative mode which is, the celebrity suggests the audience to use the endorsed product while the celebrity only appears with the product in the co-present mode.

Use of celebrity is not a new phenomenon in the advertisement field. A couple of centuries back, in Europe, Popes and Kings endorse health products. Hsu & Mcdonald (2002) stated that marketers spend a huge amount of money on celebrity endorsement contracts as they believe that celebrities are efficient representative for their product or brand. The psychology behind celebrity endorsement as Austad and Silvera (2003) understands is that celebrities are considered highly trustworthy, believable, persuasive and likeable. Farrell, et. al. (2000)

---

[51] It is estimated that top male celebrities charge anywhere between Rs 12 to 25 crore per annum for each endorsement, while their female counterparts get roughly half, according to Indian Express (May 1, 2016). On an average, top celebrities endorse as many 8-12 brands. Some economists suggest that these sky-high celebrity wages are the reason for black-money and other income tax cheatings in India.

pinpoints identification, credibility and attractiveness as the key element behind celebrity endorsements. Celebrity endorsements increase day by day as many companies use this as a strategy to attract potential buyers, compensation paid to them is also increasing (Tripp, Jensen & Carlson, 1994).

In India, it is estimated that almost 60 percent commercials use celebrities whereas it is estimated that only 20 percent commercials use celebrities at the world level; India is one of the top ten countries where celebrity endorsement is one of the popular methods of advertising (Sharma & Prabhakar, 2013). The following table shows the celebrities seen in commercials which are popular among youngsters.

No	Product	Celebrity
1.	Bru Coffee	Karthi and Kajal Aggarwal
2.	3-Roses Tea	Vikram and Trisha
3.	Aashirvaad Food Products	Sneha
4.	Sunrise Coffee (Nescafe)	Surya and Jothika
5.	Kalyan Jewellers	Aishwarya Rai
6.	Pothys Subha Muhurtham	Trisha
7.	Ramaraj Dhothis	Sarath Kumar
8.	Joy Alukkas	Vijay and his mother
9.	Chennai Silks	Ashna Zaveri
10.	RMKV Sarees	Jyothika
11.	Sri Ganapathi Silks	Poorna
12.	Sri Kumaran Thanga Malikai	Sathyaraj, Amala Paul, Saranya

The right choice of celebrity is also a key factor in creating identification and credibility of any product. For example, a comedy actor cannot endorse a sports vehicle whereas a celebrity of a different stature can do it, so also beauty products and food items. Through television, the advertisers can easily reach to the customers, within a short span of time. Nowadays, the teenagers spend their most of the time in internet, television, movies, magazines and newspaper. Marketers take advantage of young people's power to influence their family, to buy the products, to which they are attracted and it depends on gender. In the case of boys, they are mostly influenced by videogames whereas girls are attracted towards products which enhance their beauty. Sometimes, advertisements can affect the psychological level of people too, especially selfesteem and confidence level in women. For example, cosmetic advertisements can create unhappiness among young women about their bodies and faces, causing them to indulge in unhealthy eating practices leading to eating disorders.

Advertising & Marketing: Yadav (2011) identifies that advertising as a subset of marketing, is a form of communication intended to persuade people to purchase or take any action with respect to the products or the services. Today companies spend millions of rupees in advertising and marketing and therefore the competition is very high and every firm wants to sell its product and make it an established brand. Effective advertising techniques used in advertisements make a significant difference in sales. Advertising effectiveness is measured by the success of a product and how well it reaches the customers. Bishnoi (2000) who conducted a study on the impact of TV advertising on buying behaviour of rural and urban teenagers found that the rural teenagers like television advertising more than their urban counterparts. TV advertising has enhanced their involvement in product selection and purchase, they prefer to buy TV advertised products and it is helpful in buying the new products, getting the best product and also supports collective decision making. The urban teenagers also want TV advertised products even though they do not require them. They also like the advertisements of the products that they are using and believe that products are as good as expected from TV advertisements. Chang (2007) conducted a comparative study of TV commercials on rural and urban college girls in Hyderabad district indicates that the television commercials influence the living pattern and buying decision of the rural and urban college girls. The students watch different programs on various television channels, one to four hours and news, talk shows, and movies & dramas are their favourite programs.

A small study conducted in Pollachi area on 'the attitude of rural college students towards TV commercials and the related buying behaviour' by the staff and students of the psychology department in 2014 identifies the following concepts and beliefs among students.

1. **Common belief towards commercials:** Thirty percentages of students believe that even though advertisements are not very appealing if the product is good they are ready to buy it. They prefer to buy a product after enquiring the quality and rate of products. Nearly 40% of the students are attracted by the advertisement and that motivates them to buy some products. Among advertisements, the favourite actors influence their decision making irrespective of the quality of products.

2. **Attitude towards commercials:** Nearly half of the students being studied believe that advertisements are just wastage of time and disturbance that interprets the continuity of their favourite TV show or program. Also, they believe, advertisements are only meant to attract the youngsters to the product and finally resulting in the wastage of money. Few others have a belief that some advertisements are made with high technology, that can even help to increase their knowledge.

3. **Buying behaviour of students:** Twenty percent of students generally enquire about the products and go for it, on the basis of the opinion gathered. Some buy only if the products are of good quality and affordable price

4. **The decision to buy:** People in our society are so conscious about their business and it can positively affect the behaviours of status and they prefer to use branded products to show people regarding the brand image, satisfaction, and loyalty off their status symbol. Different students have different ideas or views in buying a product. Some of the decisions are made on the quality of the product, whereas some only make decisions

based on the overall attractive features of the advertisement. For few, their decisions or influenced by others opinion.

Generally, glamorous advertisements target the younger generation, therefore, very important to understand how youngsters feel about celebrity endorsement in advertisements. In view of that, a study was conducted in and around Pollachi region of Coimbatore district, collecting data from 258 adolescents (age between 18 & 21) using convenient sampling method. A small survey questionnaire prepared by the author was used to collect data. Appropriate statistical analysis was done as per the requirements. The aim of the study was to identify, how the young people, the late adolescents, perceive commercials and what are the impact of such celebrity commercials in their purchasing decision making. Specifically, the following four questions were focused.

  i) Do adolescents prefer celebrities in commercials?

  ii) What are the popular advertisements liked by them?

  iii) Do they buy a product because it is endorsed by celebrities?

  iv) What message do adolescents learn and understand which conveyed by commercials

Results and Discussion: Nearly 82 percent of the subjects were UG students and the rest PG students. The subjects belong to both the middle class and lower middle class of the economical stratum. 128 subjects were male and 130 were female. The subjects watch TV daily and they are very knowledgeable regarding the commercials.

- 53 percent of the young people being studied approve celebrities to endorse products and only 47 percent did not approve.

- Vast majority of the subjects have one or other favourite commercials which they enjoy watching in the TV or movie house.

- 27 percent of the subjects did not select any commercials as their favourite. The following table gives in rank-order, the name of commercials identified as favourite TV commercials.

- Only 22 percent of the subjects bought products because they are advertised by popular celebrities.

- The popular product being bought influenced by commercial was 'Boost'.

- Besides this gold jewellery, food items, beauty products, motorcycles are other popular products bought by them.

- Less than 9 percent of the subjects believe that the products are good because it is advertised by celebrities.

- 71 percent of the subjects do not believe a product to be good because it is advertised by celebrities.

- Nearly 5 percent of the subjects believe that commercials are by nature cheat the customers giving a false impression about the product being advertised whereas 54 percent believe that the commercials give a real picture of the products.

- 71 percent of the subjects believe that commercials are good to introduce a product in the market and 57 percent believe that the commercials give the quality and nature of the product to the customers.

- There is no noticeable gender difference in the results being analysed.

Conclusion: Advertisements do play an important role in influencing them a lot to buy products. Even though many are influenced by advertisements, some are very cautious and buy the product if they get a good and brief explanation about a product. Loyalty and relationship matter a lot and here advertisement plays a crucial role in changing behaviour. The attitudes of consumers change and vary day by day due to the easy reach of technology and other viral media. They are becoming more aware of the products that they use.

References

1. Austad and Silvera (2003). Factors predicting the effectiveness of celebrity endorsement advertisements, European Journal of Marketing, 38 (11/12), 1509-1526.

2. Benjamin, L. T., & Baker, D. B. (2004). Industrial-organizational psychology: The new psychology and the business of advertising. From séance to science: a history of the profession of psychology in America (pp.118-121). California: Wadsworth/Thomson Learning.

3. Birren, F. (1997). The power of colour: how it can reduce fatigue, Relieve Monotony, Enhance Sexuality and More, Citadel publishers.

4. Bishnoi, V. K, (2000). Impact of TV advertising on buying behaviour of rural and urban teenager. Retrieved from http://www.bvimsr.com

5. Bursik, R. J. (1984). Urban dynamics and ecological studies of delinquency. Social Forces, Vol. 63.

6. Chanda, G. & Owen, N. G. (2001). Tainted goods? Western feminism and the Asian experience. Asian Journal of Women's Studies, 7(4).

7. Chang, R, (2007) A comparative study of TV commercials on rural and urban girls colleges of Hyderabad district, Pakistan research repository. Retrieved from http://eprints.hec.gov.pk

8. Comte, A. (1856). A general view of positivism. London: Trubner & Co.

9. Croall, Hazel (2001). Understanding white collar crime, Buckingham: Open University Press.

10. Dahrendorf, R. (1959). Class and class conflict in industrial society. Stanford CA: Stanford University.

11. Datta, S. (2008). Advertisements: do they match consumer preferences? Marketing Mastermind, April, 59-62. Retrieved from http://www.bvimsr.com

12. Elwell, F. (2006). Macrosociology: four modern theorists. Paradigm Publishers.

13. Erikson, E, H. (1968). Identity: youth and crisis. NY: Norton

14. Faglio, S. (2012). Advertising: history of psychology attracting consumers. Retrieved from www.business2community.com

15. Farrell, Lisa, Roger Hartley, Gauthier Lanot, & Ian Walker. (2000). The demand for lotto: the role of conscious selection. Journal of Economic and Business Statistics 18 (2):228-241.

16. Freud, S. (1913). Totem and taboo. W.W. Norton & Co.

17. Ghurye, G. S. (1961). Caste, class, and occupation. Popular Book Depot.

18. Ginzberg, M. (2003). The psychology of society. Delhi, Khel Sahitya Kendra,.

19. Goodwin, C. J. (1999). The origins of behaviorism: a new life in advertising. A history of modern psychology (pp. 315-317). New York: John Wiley & Sons, Inc.

20. Gordon, M. (1978). Human nature, class, and ethnicity. New York: Oxford University Press.

21. Grønhaug, K., Kvitastein, O. and Grønmo, S. (1991).Factors moderating advertising effectiveness as reflected in 333 tested advertisements. Journal of Advertising Research, 31(5), 42-50.

22. Hamlin, J. (2009) The normality of crime. durkheim and erikson, Department of Sociology and Anthropology. UMD.

23. Dawkins, R. (2006). The selfish gene (30th anniversary edition). Oxford: Oxford University Press.

24. Dawkins, R. (2006). The God delusion. UK: Random House.

25. Hsu & Mcdonald (2002). An examination on multiple celebrity endorsers in advertising, Journal of Product & Brand Management, Vol. 11 Iss: 1, pp.19 – 29.

26. Jung, C. G., & Jaffe A. (1962). Memories, Dreams, Reflections. London: Collins.

27. Kakar, S. (1989). Intimate relations: exploring Indian sexuality. New Delhi: Penguin Books.

28. Kavitha, G. (2006). A study on the effectiveness of advertising techniques used in the personal care segment of women consumers. Indian Journal of Marketing, 36(8), 12-16.

29. Kleiner, K. (2004). What we gave up for colour vision. New Scientist, January 24, 2004: 12.

30. Kotwal, N., Gupta, N., and Devi, A., (2008). Impact of T.V advertisements on buying pattern of adolescent girls. Journal of Social Sciences, 16(1), 51-55.

31. Maciver, R.M. & Page, C. H. (1962). Society, an introductory analysis. Macmillan Publishers India.

32. Mahnke, F. (1996). Colour, environment, and human response: an interdisciplinary understanding of colour and its use as a beneficial element in the design of the architectural environment, John Wiley & Sons.

33. Marshall, G. (1998). Taboo. A Dictionary of Sociology. 1998. Retrieved from encyclopaedia http://www.encyclopedia.com

34. McCracken, G. (1989). Who is the celebrity endorser? cultural foundation of the endorsement process, Journal of Consumer Research, 16 (3), 310-321.

35. McCracken, G. (1989). Who is the celebrity endorser? cultural foundations of the endorsement process, Journal of Consumer Research, Vol. 16, December, pp. 310-21.

36. McMillan, D.W., & Chavis, D.M. (1986). Sense of community: a definition and theory. American Journal of Community Psychology, 14(1).

37. Ortega, J. (1957). Man and people. New York: W. W. Norton.

38. Parsons, T. & Shils, E. (1951). Toward a general theory of action. Harvard University Press.

39. Pathak, V. (2013). Fashion among students, posted in Essays, paragraphs and articles. Retrieved from www.importantindia.com

40. Pethiyagoda, K. (2015). Indian tolerance: the view from outside, The World Post, 11 September.

41. Rebecca, Willis (2011). Why black is addictive. Intelligent life magazine, November/December 2011.

42. Ritberger, C. (2005). What colour is your personality, Hay House Publishers.

43. Robin. (2014). What is colour-blindness and the different types? Colour vision testing, retrieved from http://colorvisiontesting.com

44. Santhosh Kumar K, & Velavan. (2013). Impact of TV advertising on buying behaviours of rural and urban college students with special reference to Coimbatore, Erode and Tirupur Districts in Tamilnadu. Research Journal of Social Science and Management. Vol 3, No 5.

45. Schneider, F. W., Gruman, J. A., & Coutts, L. M. (2012). Applied social psychology: understanding and addressing social and practical problems. Los Angeles: Sage.

46. Sharma, P. & Prabhakar, A. (2013). Role of celebrity advertising in India, BICON-2013 peer-reviewed conference proceeding.

47. Sorokin, P. (1938). Social and culture dynamics. New York: H. Fertig.

48. Sorokin, P. (1970). Social and cultural dynamics: a study of change in major systems of art, truth, ethics, law and social relationships. Boston: Extending Horizons Books.

49. Spengler, O. (1991). The decline of the west: an abridged edition. Oxford University Press.

50. Taleja, N. (2008). Impact of celebrity endorsements on overall brands. Retrieved from www.coolavenues.com

51. Tonnies. (1957). Community and society. Dover Publications.

52. Torrey, E. F. (1986). Witchdoctors and psychiatrists. NJ: Jason Aronson.

53. Toynbee, A. (1946). Study of history. Oxford University Press.

54. Tripp, C., Jensen, D. T. & Carlson, L. (1994). The effect of multiple product endorsements by celebrities on consumers' attitude and intentions, Journal of Consumer Research, Vol. 20, pp. 535-547.

55. Watson, L. (1995). Dark nature: a natural history of evil. London: Hodder & Stoughton.

56. Bartollas. C. & Contrad, J.P. (1992). Introduction to corrections, Harpercollins College Div.

57. Paranjape, N.V. (2001). Criminology & penology, Central Law Publications.

58. Grabosky, P. & Smith, R. (1998). Crime in the digital age, Sydney: Federation Press.

59. Krishna Kumar (2016). Internet addiction's a public health issue, The Hindu – Business Line, July 15.

60. Waugh, R. (2012). Internet addiction can cause physical damage to the brain, Retrieved from http://www.dailymail.co.uk

61. Yadav A, (2011). Advertisements and their impact on consumer buying behaviour. Retrieved from www.studymode.com

62. Zinkhan, G. M. (1994). Advertising ethics: emerging methods and trends. Journal of Advertising, 23 (3), 1-4.

About the Author

Janetius is an Indian Psychologist, Administrator and Multidisciplinary Researcher, graduated from De La Salle University, Philippines. In the last two decades he has worked in the Philippines, in Africa, in India and for a short stint in Australia, teaching, training and leading people from various segments and nations. He is an ardent researcher in the field of culture, behaviour, psychology, education and indigenous studies.

Notes...

_____

Notes...
_____